LOCOMOTION PAPERS

THE GARSTANG & KNOTT END RAILWAY

by

R. W. RUSH and M. PRICE

THE OAKWOOD PRESS

© Oakwood Press 1985

First edition 1964
ISBN 0 85361 318 4

All rights reserved. No part of this book may be reproduced or transmitted in any form or by any means, electronic or mechanical, including photo-copying, recording or by any information storage and retrieval system, without permission from the Publisher in writing.

Published by
The OAKWOOD PRESS
P.O. Box 122 Headington Oxford

PREFACE

A number of articles have been written from time to time by various eminent authorities on this small independent railway, but for most people it has remained a little-known undertaking. As such it was a strange coincidence that two people should simultaneously have embarked on a comprehensive history of the line. Once this was discovered, the obvious answer was collaboration, and it is to be hoped that the result will adequately fill the gap.

At all events the authors have been to considerable lengths to unravel the somewhat obscure history of the company. Unfortunately the Derby Works fire of 1951 caused a great deal of useful material to be lost. Hence there is a paucity of official records and it has been very difficult to obtain confirmation of many details. Grateful acknowledgments are due to the writers of the various articles enumerated in the Bibliography, and to the kindness of the locomotive builders—Robert Stephenson and Hawthorns Ltd. (who hold the records of Manning Wardle & Co.) and Hudswell Clarke & Co. Ltd., both of whom have been extremely helpful in providing details of the locomotives. Valuable assistance in this field has come additionally from the Birmingham Locomotive Club, whilst material has also been provided by Lens of Sutton, the *Lancashire Evening Post*, Mr. Eric Mason and Dr. G. Reed, the latter supplying a copy of the most interesting 1908 1d. Guide to the railway. Finally, thanks must be extended to the Public Relations and Publicity Officer, British Railways (L.M.R.) (for the loan of the official station plans from which the track layout diagrams were made), to the Registrar of Companies, the Public Records Office, the Archivist of the British Transport Commission, and the Public Relations Officer, L.M.R., Manchester, for facilities to travel on "the Pilling Pig."

Apart from the historical side, this book has been compiled with an eye to railway modelling. Thus it is hoped that the various drawings will prove useful to anyone intending to make the line their modelling subject. As regards the passenger and goods rolling stock, the drawings cannot be guaranteed accurate in all dimensions for the reason stated above, but they are believed to be as near the truth as is possible under the circumstances.

ROBERT W. RUSH,   MARTIN R. CONNOR PRICE,

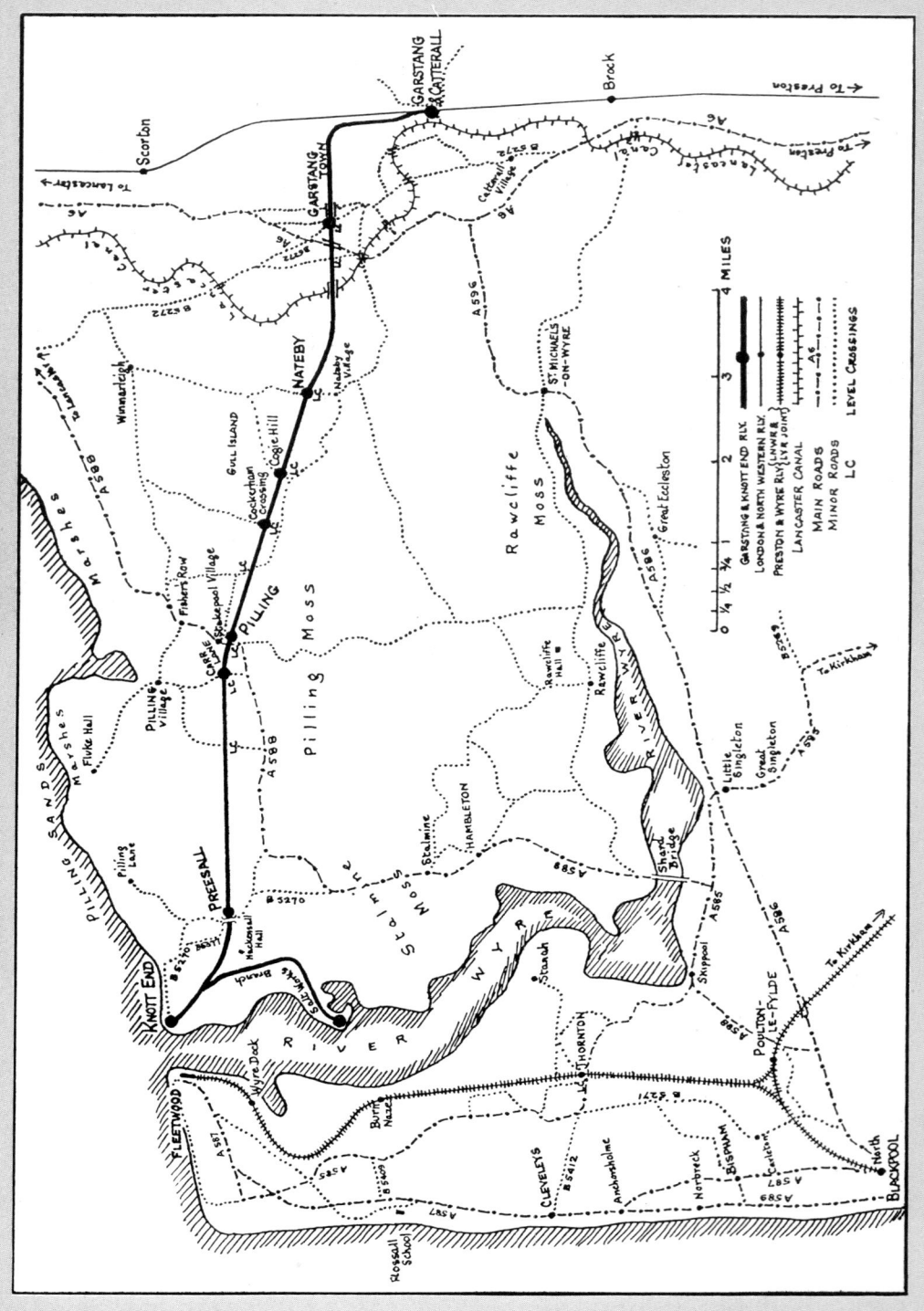

1. INTRODUCTION

To most people, particularly those in the southern parts of these islands, Lancashire is a mass of dismal towns, full of gloomy mills and dark houses, overcast by an everlasting pall of smoke—and where it does nothing but rain. Such people have never seen Lancashire, for their opinion is a gross libel on one of England's greatest counties. Less than one-third of its area is industrial, and even in this part— mainly in the south and south-east districts—it is far from being the hell-on-earth which it is made out to be. Gloomy mills and dark houses there are, true enough, but few towns are more than a mile or so from green open fields, and in the east the rolling hills and clear fresh moorland air of the Pennines. The northern half of the county, above a line drawn from the Ribble Estuary through Blackburn and Burnley to the Yorkshire border, is as pleasant a land as can be found anywhere in England, and this broad agricultural area spreads also into the south-west, almost to the borders of Liverpool. North of the Ribble estuary a flat tract of land, almost devoid of hills, juts out westwards with the port of Fleetwood at its tip. This, the Fylde, as it is called, covers upwards of a hundred square miles of rich agricultural land, and it is with the northern part of the Fylde with which we are concerned in this book. It is thinly populated, but there are a number of small pleasant villages nestling in leafy lanes, and many farmsteads scattered about the land. There are, too, several large mansions, in which dwelt, in days gone by, the squires of the district—the large landowners from whom the smaller farmers rented their land; but nowadays most farmers own their own fields, and several of the mansions are now gone, or turned to other purposes—Rossall Hall, for example, near Fleetwood, has been for many years a famous Public School. Two of the former squires played a large part in this story, as we shall see.

The market town, to which most of the produce of this district is sent, is Garstang, which lies astride the main A6 trunk road to Carlisle, though for many years past the town itself has been bypassed by a new section of road which avoids its narrow main street. Garstang is an old town, with a population of some 3,000, having several old and quaint buildings, and a market cross which dominates the main street. It has too a flourishing cattle and produce market, held on Thursdays, which attracts farmers from miles around, both from the Fylde and the hill-country to the east. Though readily accessible by road, the town is not well served by rail, for its station (Garstang & Catterall) is 2½ miles away to the south-east, on the former London & North Western main line to Scotland.

This northern portion of the Fylde was formerly known as Amounderness, though this name has largely fallen into disuse. In the early part of the nineteenth century it was a vast peat bog, the coastal fringes of which were frequently under water at high tide. Indeed, to this day, the main road from Lancaster to Blackpool which runs along part of this coast, is sometimes impassable at high tide. To the north of the road, the sea marshes are a favourite haunt of anglers and wild-fowlers, and the treacherous bogs have claimed many victims of both sports. Not only in recent times have the marshes had their prey, for Amounderness has had its share of history. There were many skirmishes here during the Civil War; Lord Derby and Sir Thomas Tyldesley (of Fox Hall, Blackpool) landed at Knott End from the Isle of Man in 1651, and marched on Chester, where Lord Derby was made prisoner. Sir Thomas did not fare so well, for he was killed in the Battle of Wigan, and a monument in that town commemorates him. During the same year, a Spanish ship ran aground on Pilling Sands, and became a bone of contention between Cavaliers and Roundheads until at last it was set on fire by the former party. Several survivors of the ship's crew settled in the district. Again, during the Jacobite rebellion of 1745, a number of Highlanders fleeing after the Battle of Preston, were lost in the bogs of Amounderness. In later years, the coastal villages took to smuggling and wrecking—which trades one mostly associates with Cornwall—and there are many stories told of dark deeds on the marshes in the dead of night.

An old map of the district, dated 1818, shows a large open area at the mouth of the River Wyre, marked laconically " Rabbit Warren "; though on the opposite shore a tiny village is shown, named Knott End. The Squire of Rossall Hall, in whose demesne the " Rabbit Warren " lay, by name Sir Peter Hesketh Fleetwood, conceived the idea that the broad estuary of the Wyre could become a great port, and a good deal of his private fortune was spent in accomplishing his dream. The first houses of the town of Fleetwood were erected in 1836, and the main streets, all converging on a grassy mound near the foreshore (now a public park known as The Mount) were marked out with a plough in the sandy soil. Building proceeded apace, and though the first quays were built along the river in 1840, it was not until some thirty years later that the port became really established. Since that day it has expanded and improved, and the establishment of a fishing fleet, and the Isle of Man Steam Packet Co.'s steamer services to the Island Kingdom, brought prosperity to Fleetwood. It always suffered, however, from the sluggishness of the River Wyre, continually depositing large quantities of silt in the channel, which needed frequent dredging. In 1962 the steamer services have had to be discontinued, having only been maintained with difficulty for several years ; only by the expenditure of a colossal amount of money can the silting of the channel be overcome, and moreover, the quays having been in use for upwards of a century, much work is needed to bring them up to present day standards. This work the town is unable to meet, and though representations have been made to the Government for assistance in the modernisation plans, no help has been forthcoming. The fishing fleet, however, remains faithful to the port, and for the past thirty years or so, Fleetwood has set itself out to become a holiday resort, a project in which it has been largely successful.

2. THE COMING OF THE RAILWAY

It might be thought at first glance that Fleetwood would be the natural outlet for the produce of Amounderness, since it stands immediately opposite Knott End, but unfortunately it is separated by some four or five hundred yards of estuary which cannot be bridged without seriously obstructing the fairway to shipping, and the nearest bridge is seven miles upstream. (Even that was not in existence at the time when the railway was proposed.) Fleetwood Corporation established a steam ferry across the estuary for foot passengers and bicycles only; owing to the great variation in tide levels, it was not found practicable to make suitable landing stages for vehicular traffic, which still has to go round by Shard Bridge, a detour of some 13 miles. So, if one realises that this ferry was a comparatively modern innovation, and that Shard Bridge was not built in the 1860's, it will be easy to see why the farmers of the district turned their eyes eastwards when seeking an outlet for their goods. The local roads were narrow and winding, so progress with farm carts to Garstang Market was slow and troublesome, and not unnaturally, a railway was proposed to link the district with Garstang, and so to the rest of the county by way of Preston.

The railway was the brain-child of the local landowners, chief among them being the Squire of Rawcliffe, Wilson ffrance. After what seemed almost interminable discussions, one John Addis, who was ffrance's bailiff, was given the job of arranging the whole affair, and he got in touch with an engineer named James Tolmé, between them producing a workable plan to connect Knott End with the L.N.W.R. at Garstang and Catterall station. Armed with these plans, Wilson ffrance proceeded to canvass the local gentry with a view to forming a company to put the project into effect. Eventually, in December 1863 a glowing prospectus was issued, naming six directors —Col. James Bourne, Julian Augustus Tarner, Richard Bennett, Henry Gardner, John Russell, and James Overend—and setting out in their name the proposals they had agreed upon. The company was to be called the Garstang & Knot-end Railway (note the spelling). It claimed that the proposed line would be the most direct connection between Fleetwood and the industrial areas of Lancashire and Yorkshire; that eventually it could become part of a new direct route between the Wyre and the Humber. (How this was to be accomplished with the great mass of the Bowland Fells standing directly in the way beyond Garstang, is best left to the imagination—certainly the prospectus was discreetly silent on the subject.) The Company's capital was given as £60,000, and the length of the railway as $11\frac{1}{2}$ miles between Knott End and the junction with the L.N.W.R. There was also a veiled proposal that harbour facilities should be constructed at Knott End. This latter clause stirred up the interest of the Lancashire & Yorkshire and London & North Western Railways, for as joint owners of the Preston & Wyre Railway, they had a proprietary interest in the port of Fleetwood, and indeed had at that same time a Bill in Parliament for the building of further dock facilities there. Naturally, talk of a rival port across the river set them by the ears, and they announced that they would fight the Garstang & Knot-end proposals with all the power at their command.

A Select Committee of the House of Lords was appointed in March 1864 to examine the proposals on both sides. Giving evidence before the Committee, the Garstang party climbed down considerably from their high perch, and avowed solemnly that "the line was a simple and unpretending railway, designed solely for the accommodation of the local traffic of the district", and pointed out that no allocation of capital had been made whatsoever towards any harbour works; indeed with the limited sum of £60,000 such works would be impossible. The L. & Y. and L.N.W.R. asserted that the area was thinly populated, and could hardly expect to support a railway, even of a local character, but the G. & K.E. stressed the thriving agriculture of the district, which they maintained was the real reason for the line, passenger traffic being of a very minor nature. On these assurances, the two big companies withdrew their opposition, but maintained a watching brief in case any attempt were made to push the harbour proposals through at the last minute. The Select Committee reported in favour of the Bill, which was then passed to the Commons, and received the Royal Assent on 30 June 1864, with a five-year limit for construction, a clause which was to cause no end of trouble, as will be seen.

It should be mentioned that although we have described the area as being a vast peat bog in the early part of the century, enormous strides have been taken for its reclamation in the ensuing years. An old local saying was that " Pilling Moss, like God's grace, knows no bounds." Further to the north-east lay another bog, in the estate of the Duke of Hamilton, who in 1835 had started a scheme of reclamation. The Duke set up a pottery on his estate for the sole purpose of making drain pipes, and having first dug a ditch for six miles to the coast near where Glasson Dock now stands, laid down no less than 109 miles of drain pipes to connect the various parts of his land to this ditch, effectively draining off the underlying water from the bog, and paving the way for making valuable land from it.

The Duke's example was noted by the Squire of Rawcliffe, Wilson ffrance, and he proceeded to do the same with his own share of the useless bog, and with the co-operation of the adjoining landowners, the greater part of Amounderness was so drained. A main ditch was dug, commencing in Rawcliffe Moss, and traversing the other two great bogs, Stalmine Moss and Pilling Moss, reached the sea near Pilling village. Land drains were laid to this from all parts of the area, in similar manner to the Duke of Hamilton's scheme, and a sluice-gate was built at the seaward end to prevent the sea flooding into the ditch. When most of the water had been drained off from beneath the peat, the latter was sliced off and stacked, the whole land dug over thoroughly, and new roads made to a standard width of 21 feet. The roads were raised above the level of the land, much of the surplus peat being used to bank them up.

This whole operation took many years, even with the wholehearted co-operation of everyone in the district, but it began to show astonishing results by the time that the railway Bill was passed. Crops of grain, potatoes and vegetables were well established, and thriving. A small area of bogland remained unreclaimed near Cogie Hill; for some inexplicable reason, this bit just refused to drain off. This was known locally as "Gull Island", as it became a home for a large colony of seabirds, and was declared a sanctuary for them. A warden was appointed, paid by the local landowners, to watch over the area during the nesting season and protect the birds from the depredations of wildfowlers and egg-hunters. Incidentally, Cogie Hill was a misnomer, if ever there was one; there was not a hill in sight.

So far, so good. The Act had been passed, and there was nothing (in theory) to prevent the company getting on with the job of building the railway, but in practice it was a very different kettle of fish. It had been arranged during the preliminary discussions with the local farmers that they would sell the necessary land to the company at agricultural value, and would take payment in shares instead of cash. But now difficulties arose; some went back on their word and demanded payment in cash, while some wanted to substitute an alternative strip of land in place of that planned. As this would have contravened the Act, and thus necessitated an application to Parliament for deviations, there was naturally much argument and delay before anything could be done. In the end, the farmers handed over the land originally earmarked for the purpose, but the protracted legal proceedings and the demands for cash payments which were persisted in, ran away with a considerable proportion of the company's capital, with disastrous results. To a large extent, the blame must lie with the directorate, none of whom had any specialised knowledge of railways, and who were, in any case, too dilatory in exercising their powers under the Act.

Wilson ffrance, who had been the strong man of the party in the early days, was by now too old to take an active part, and the Chairman, Mr. Tarner, had not the experience of leadership to maintain a firm control of his Board. It would seem also that James Tolmé had not much say in the matter; though the firm in which he was the junior partner—Galbraith & Tolmé, of London—were named as the company's engineers, he would appear to have left matters very much in the hands of the contractors, and for some considerable time there was no resident engineer to be in general charge of the works. The first contractor, Wheatley Kirk, of Manchester, resigned in April 1865, having succeeded in preparing only half a mile of the roadbed at the Garstang end. Between him and the directors there was a long and bitter wrangle over the amount of money allotted to him to carry on the work, and as this was eventually not forthcoming, he threw in his hand. The company released him from his obligations under his contract, but could find no other contractor willing to take over the prevailing circumstances. So a partnership of three shareholders was formed—Allen, Noble and Addis—to carry on. Incidentally, this Addis was the same person who had originally prepared the plans for the railway some five years earlier, and who was now Secretary of the company. He, it seems, managed to get hold of an engineer, one William Hamand, and appointed him to take charge on the site, under the general (but remote) control of Galbraith & Tolmé. None of the three partners in this new firm had had any previous experience of railway construction work, and the acquisition of Hamand, who had a little, was considered a good stroke of business. Addis and Hamand seem to have struck up a particular friendship, which had some bearing on subsequent events.

Little progress had been made by May 1867, and the company was compelled to appeal to Parliament for an extension of time till 1870, which was granted. In this same month, it came to the ears of certain shareholders that Addis and Hamand had been on a fact-finding mission in Wales, examining narrow-gauge railways, and they had decided mutually to construct the Garstang & Knott-end Railway as a 3′ 0″ gauge line, in direct contravention of the Act, wherein it was laid down that it should be of standard gauge, with direct connection to the L.N.W.R. lines at Garstang and Catterall. Certain of the directors had been briefed by Addis in the pros and cons of narrow gauge railways, and they were said to be in favour of this scheme. Having got wind of these machinations, a number of shareholders formed themselves into the Knott End Railway Shareholders' Association, bent on examining closely any agreements entered into by the directors and contractors. Tarner, as chairman of the company, had rather a hot time between the directors on the one hand, and the shareholders on the other. It was a delicate situation; one faction determined to stick to the strict conditions of the Act, and the other with its specious arguments for a narrow gauge line, amongst which the considerable saving in money was the main point. Since the company's finances were in none too healthy a state, this argument carried a great deal of weight; but the Shareholders' Association was determined in their stand on the interpretation of the Act, making their main argument the great inconvenience which would be caused by a break of gauge at the junction with the L.N.W.R. Moreover, they pointed out, non-compliance with the terms of the Act would involve them in prolonged litigation, which cost money, so what was the point of saving it now, only to squander it in unnecessary legal fees in two or three years' time—especially if the loss of the (hypothetical) case would mean conversion of the whole line back from narrow gauge to standard? After a long wrangle the Association won the day, and the directors agreed to carry out the works as originally planned. As a result of this, Addis resigned his post as secretary of the company, and was succeeded by James Noble.

Three years had already passed out of the five allotted, and all there was to show for it was half a mile of roadbed. One of the partners in the contracting firm, Allen, resigned. The reason was not stated, but it is reasonable to assume that it had something to do with the abortive narrow gauge scheme. In his place, the company were lucky for once, in obtaining the service of George Bush, an engineer who had nearly thirty years' experience in building railways, both at home and abroad. At last a capable man had been found. From then onwards things began to move, but owing to all the financial quibbling, and the vacillations of the directorate, the company found itself extremely short of capital, a large proportion of the original £60,000 having gone, with little or nothing to show for it. At a stormy meeting in December 1867, it was decided reluctantly that the $4\frac{1}{2}$ miles of line between Pilling and Knott End should not be built for the time being, leaving the truncated section between the junction and Pilling, 7 miles in length, as the immediate objective. Even so, by the time of the opening, the total cost had reached £150,000—this astronomical figure being all the more surprising in that there were no engineering works of any magnitude on the whole line ; apart from the first $2\frac{3}{4}$ miles from the junction to the point where it crossed the Lancaster Canal, east of Garstang, it was laid on the surface of the land and was practically dead level. Also from the canal to Pilling it was dead straight, apart from a slight deviation near the former point made for the convenience of two landowners—the railway then forming the boundary between their properties.

At the same meeting, it was decided to lease the line to the contractors, who agreed to work it for 50% of the nett profits, provided that the company would supply the rolling stock and officials. In June 1869 Hamand, who had more or less tacitly been appointed Locomotive, Carriage and Wagon Superintendent (though no such post appeared in the company's records) ordered four coaches from the Metropolitan Railway Carriage & Wagon Co., of Birmingham, in readiness for the opening of the line. Early in 1870, the builders notified Hamand that the coaches were ready, and would be delivered to Garstang on receipt of the company's cheque. This put the cat among the pigeons with a vengeance, for the cheque could not be met, and the coaches remained in the works at Birmingham, the builders being forced to charge interest on the purchase price, plus rental for storage until such time as the coaches could be paid for. In order that something could be done to break the impasse, fourteen shareholders formed themselves into the Garstang Rolling Stock Company, with a capital of £5,000, the date of incorporation being 12th October 1870. This company put up the purchase price (plus the extras) for the four coaches, and agreed to lease them to the railway for £100 per annum. They also negotiated the purchase of 24 wagons and two brake vans, which were leased to the railway on similar terms.

Hamand had also ordered a locomotive from Black, Hawthorn & Co., of Gateshead, this being one of the firm's stock designs, an 0-4-2 saddle tank, which rejoiced in the name of " Hebe ". There is no evidence to show why this particular name was chosen ; it had no connection in any shape or form with the Garstang & Knot-end Railway, and does not appear to be a name previously used by the makers. In Greek mythology, Hebe was the Goddess of Youth. There may be some connection here, but if so, it is very obscure.

The same state of affairs pertained to the locomotive as to the coaches—the railway was unable to pay. In this case, Black, Hawthorn & Co., possibly not being aware of the financial state of the G. & K.E.R., had rather rashly delivered the engine to Garstang before asking for payment, and the railway, following the old adage that a bird in the hand is worth two in the bush, promptly took possession of it and put it to work. Somebody eventually paid the piper, but there is considerable doubt as to who that somebody was ; it was definitely not the Garstang Rolling Stock Company. It is equally certain that " Hebe " was never the property of the G. & K.E.R. In May 1871, the directors received, and accepted, an offer from the British Wagon Co. to pay for the engine and lease it to the railway for a period of seven years, the railway to pay a sum which would cover the initial cost, plus interest at $2\frac{1}{2}\%$, in seven annual payments ; at the end of that time, the engine would be their own property. In spite of this, a shareholder named Walter Mayhew forwarded a cheque to the directors in July for the full purchase price, with an agreement to lease the engine to them for an unlimited period, with a view to eventual purchase. Whether

Mayhew was acting for himself, or on behalf of another body is not clear, but his cheque was accepted, and the agreement with the British Wagon Co. cancelled. Whatever the truth of the matter, " Hebe " was working on the line prior to the official opening in December 1870. It was not, however, the first locomotive to run on the line, this doubtful honour falling to an unspecified L.N.W.R. engine hired in September 1870 to test the track and bridges.

It should be mentioned that as the first extension of Parliamentary powers for construction of the line expired in June 1870, a second application had to be made. This was granted for a further twelve months, but not without some caustic comments about the unconscionable time needed to build a mere seven miles of railway. The company thought it expedient to let the matter of the remaining $4\frac{1}{2}$ miles to Knott End remain in abeyance for the time being, though they got an assurance that should they re-apply for powers to finish the line in the not too distant future, there was no reason why they should not be granted, provided that the company could show an appreciable improvement in their financial position.

3. THE FIRST STAGE — DISASTER

The official opening of the line took place on 14th December 1870, without the usual pomp and ceremony associated with such events, in view of the financial position. This did not prevent a celebration dinner being held at the Royal Oak Hotel in Garstang, which was attended by the directors, officials, contractors, and the more influential shareholders, including the members of the Garstang Rolling Stock Company. The chairman, Mr. J. A. Tarner, gave thanks to the directors, particularly those who had dipped deep into their own pockets, at considerable personal sacrifice, to find the additional capital necessary to complete the line to Pilling. Even so, they had been forced to abandon the original project to reach the mouth of the Wyre at Knott End, though he hoped that in the near future it would be possible to revive that scheme, and bring the line to its logical terminus. No mention was made of the earlier dalliance on the part of the directorate, nor of the warring factions amongst them!

Incidentally, though not officially open until the 14th December, traffic had actually been operating over the line, as per public timetable, for nine days previously. This public timetable was a masterpiece of ingenuity ; it provided a service of nine trains in each direction between the junction and Garstang Town, three of which ran through to or from Pilling, and in spite of making reasonable connection with the main-line trains of the L.N.W.R., the whole service could be worked by one engine only—which was all they had, anyway. All trains were " mixed "—goods and passenger together. All trains also carried first- and third-class passengers (though third class was called " Parliamentary " in the official notices.) There was no service at all on Sundays. Thus " Hebe " was expected to be in service for some sixteen hours daily, leaving virtually only Sundays for repairs and maintenance. It says much for the workmanship of " Hebe's " builders that under these strenuous conditions nothing serious went wrong with her for upwards of eighteen months, in spite of the fact that boiler washouts were unknown, and regular inspection was not carried out. This is borne out by the fact that in January 1872, we find the secretary (James Noble) being instructed to contact the District Running Superintendent of the L.N.W.R. at Preston to try and arrange for monthly boiler inspections, and also to obtain "a rubber hosepipe, or other suitable appliance " for washing out the boiler. Whether this regular inspection was arranged or not with the authorities at Preston is very doubtful, for some two months later the company found itself without an engine at all, so it is hardly likely. Three new boiler tubes were supplied by Black, Hawthorn & Co. in March 1872, and in the following June, Noble was instructed to visit Sharp Stewart's works at Manchester to try and obtain nine more. Though it is not officially stated, it seems likely that Black, Hawthorn had supplied the three boiler tubes on credit, and not receiving payment, had refused to supply any more ; else why go to another firm to buy nine boiler tubes for an engine not of that firm's manufacture ? It may be quite common practice in these days, but at that time it was not ; usually any replacement parts were supplied by the builders as a matter of course.

A notice was posted at the headquarters of the railway (at Garstang Town station) on 5th March 1872, to the effect that all traffic would be suspended from Monday 11th March to Wednesday the 13th inclusive, while the engine underwent " thorough repairs ". (Apparently, this could only refer to the replacement of the first three boiler tubes.) On the following Thursday, traffic was resumed as usual. This contretemps stimulated the directors to confer with George Bush (who was operating the line on behalf of the contractors, according to the agreement) as to the possibilities of obtaining a second engine on hire-purchase for £500–£600, but unfortunately this came to nothing. The owners of "Hebe", presumably the Walter Mayhew previously mentioned, having received no payment for the hire of the engine for several months previously, withdrew the locomotive from service. As from early April 1872, the Garstang & Knot-end Railway was virtually closed. The secretary was given six months' notice, the track was fenced off at the junction, and "Hebe" was taken to Garstang and Catterall goods yard, where she was put in a siding, tallowed down, and sheeted over. The question of the nine boiler tubes requested in the following June, presumably to put the engine in good order again, was never resolved. "Hebe" thus faded out of the picture, and what happened to her subsequently, will be seen later. Orders went out that all spare brass and iron anywhere along the line should be brought in to Garstang with a view to sale.* Dwellers in the railway-owned cottages who had got in arrears with rent (quite a considerable number) were ordered to "pay up or else". Most managed to pay, but several were forcibly evicted.

Occasional use was made of the railway with horse traction during the next three years, but this was entirely sporadic, and was in no way a regular service. A certain "Bob the Barber", of Garstang, made a steady living by meeting all L.N.W.R. trains at Garstang and Catterall Station with a horse and cart, in which he conveyed passengers to the town at 8d. per head. For such as required it, he threw in a shave at his shop free.

Harking back to the time of opening the line, the chronic lack of funds led to all sorts of unorthodox, and indeed dangerous, practices in the daily working. To begin with, the line was not signalled, and was not required to be, as it was worked on the "one-engine-in-steam" principle. Wagons were left at any convenient point on the line, and picked up on the return journey, so that it would be not uncommon to see five or six wagons being pushed along in front of the train (quite often uncoupled) besides the normal train being hauled. Farm carts from miles around blocked the goods yards at Pilling and Garstang Town, and it became a sort of "free for all" whenever a train came in. Anyone who could jump on to a moving wagon while it was being shunted was tacitly agreed to have won the right to load that wagon, and with this shocking practice it was not surprising that many accidents occurred. Let it be said now that it was the farmers themselves who started this dangerous practice, and not the railway company, though

*It is said that quite a rumpus developed as this auction (by Dr. Reed's grandfather incidentally!) was wrongly authorised.

the latter were to blame for their lack of organisation, and for making only half-hearted efforts to stop it. After a few months it was the accepted thing, and no one on either side cared anything for safety. Richard Bradshaw, of Pilling, had a leg cut off through falling under a moving wagon, and died soon afterwards. This was early in 1871, only two months after the line was opened. A particularly sad case occurred in the following June, to William Percy of Stakepool. This elderly man who was a direct descendant of the Lords Percy of Northumberland (one of whom was the famous " Henry Hotspur ", killed in the Battle of Shrewsbury in 1403) had been evicted from his cottage by the Squire of Parrox Hall. Percy declared that though evicted from his home, no one was going to turn him off his land which he had farmed for so many years, squire or no squire. He was a very popular man, while the Squire was not ; so several of his friends in the district connived at his antics to defeat authority. They got him a small wooden hut, which they fitted with wheels (one version of the story says that it was a bathing machine filched in the dead of night from Fleetwood beach). When turned off his land by the squire's bailiff, he would wheel his hut away without protest, but in the dark hours, it would be wheeled back again. This happened so often that the Squire finally gave up in disgust, and Percy was allowed to remain on his beloved land, greatly to the delight of the villagers. He was a great character, full of fun and native wit, and a great walker—when nearly sixty years of age he beat the stage coach from Liverpool to Garstang by over an hour, entirely on foot. One day in June 1871, when taking some of his produce to Pilling station, he was unfortunate enough to get caught between two moving wagons, and was crushed to death. The coroner had some very forcible things to say about the practice of jumping wagons, and ordered it to cease forthwith—but no notice was taken of him. A similar occurrence at Garstang Town in March 1871, involving a young employee of the company, was not dealt with so harshly by the Garstang coroner. He declared that " too much blame should not be attached to the railway company owing to the parlous state of their finances". This was small comfort to the relatives of the victim. The practice of jumping wagons went on unabated until the virtual closure of the line in 1872. The Garstang and Knott-end Railway had earned itself a very bad reputation—not by any means unjustly.

14   The Garstang & Knott End Railway

A fine early view of Garstang Town Station in the early period of the railway.   *R. Kidner*

A fair number of passengers waiting for the train which is just pulling in to Pilling Station in 1920s before the second platform was constructed.   *R. Kidner*

4. THE SECOND STAGE — CONSOLIDATION

In 1874, the company tried to introduce a Bill in Parliament for the sale of the railway, but as no purchasers were named, this contravened Standing Orders of the House of Lords, and the Bill was thrown out. Overtures were made to both the London & North Western and Lancashire & Yorkshire Railways, but both refused to take over the line under any circumstances, either separately or jointly. Towards the end of the same Parliamentary session, the Bill was re-introduced in the names of the principal debenture-holders, but was still deemed to be contrary to Standing Orders. To end the impasse, some of the debenture holders filed a suit in Chancery for the compulsory winding-up of the company. As things turned out, this was the best thing that could have happened, for the Court appointed an official receiver, and from that time forward the finances of the G. & K.E.R. took a turn for the better. Under the able guidance of the Receiver, the debenture holders first purchased a secondhand engine named " Union "—a Manning Wardle 0-4-0 saddle tank, which had been built in 1868 for a contractor named James Pilling, and employed in the construction of the Lancashire Union Railway (Chorley–Blackburn), hence its name. With this engine goods traffic was re-opened on 23rd February 1875, and passenger traffic on the 17th of the following April. Gradually, over the next five years, the whole of the track was relaid, and the stations refurbished, entirely out of revenue.

It was increasingly obvious, however, that the service could not be maintained with one engine, as had been attempted in the earlier years, but it was equally obvious that the impoverished state of the railway's finances could not stand such a capital outlay. The Garstang Rolling Stock Company had enough on its plate as it was—the coaches and wagons were its sole assets, since no payments for hire had been received for four years, and what little remained of the company's capital must obviously be used to maintain the rolling stock in good order. Another engine was a necessity, but neither of the existing companies was in a position to purchase one, even secondhand. The only solution was to form yet a third company specifically for the purpose, and so the Garstang & Knott End Railway Engine Company came into being on 9th December 1875, with a nominal capital of £2,000, subscribed by eight directors, only one of whom (James Collinson) was a director of the Rolling Stock Co.

It is important to keep these three companies in mind, for the names are very much alike, and it is easy to confuse them. When a fourth company came into being twenty years later, the confusion became even worse, especially, as we shall see in due course, the fourth company operated the railway under the name of the first, though strictly speaking, that company had ceased to exist! For that matter, so had the two intervening companies. However, to get back to the events of 1875, the Engine Company purchased a new locomotive from Hudswell, Clarke & Rogers, of Leeds, an 0-6-0 saddle tank which had been built for stock earlier in the same year; it was given the name of " Farmers Friend ". This engine was hired to the railway for the sum of £78 per annum. It possessed a whistle which emitted a peculiarly piercing shriek, and in consequence soon became known as the " Pilling Pig "—a name which survives to this day, for the daily goods train which still meanders down the line is known by the same soubriquet.*

With two engines to work the traffic, things began to improve rapidly, and for the first time in the railway's history the locomotives could receive regular routine attention, and thus be kept in good order. Traffic increased, and a new period of prosperity dawned—though the railway was not out of the wood yet, by any means. A proper organisation of the goods yards did away with the iniquitous " wagon-jumping" capers, and no more were odd wagons left lying around in odd places, to the general danger of every train. Moreover, with the regular use of two engines, the Board of Trade regulations demanded proper signalling, and this was installed, though except at the junction and Garstang Town, was not of main-line standard. A modified type of block working was also introduced.

In 1880, the arrears of rent for the rolling stock were paid off, and so the subsidiary Rolling Stock Co. was enabled to purchase additional wagons, which were badly needed, and lease them to the railway on the same terms. In 1884, the finances of the company had improved to such an extent that it was possible to purchase " Farmers Friend " outright from the owners, who in turn purchased another new 0-6-0 saddle tank to replace " Union ", which was really too small for the work required of it, though it had given yeoman service in time of need. The new engine, which was also a Hudswell Clarke product, was delivered in 1885, the builders taking " Union " in part exchange. It was given the name "Hope". (Was this an ironic comment on the state of the railway's finances ?) This engine never became the property of the

*Another nickname for the route was the " Pig and Whistle Railway."

G. & K.E.R., but was on hire from the Engine Co. until 1898, when it was taken back by the builders in part exchange for yet another new one.

Also, in 1883, the railway found it possible to buy the rolling stock outright, and in consequence, the Garstang Rolling Stock Company, having outlived its usefulness was formally dissolved under Section 7(4) of the Companies Act 1880, by notice in the *London Gazette* of 15th January 1884. With the winding up of this company, George Bush severed his connection with the G. & K.E.R., having been intimately concerned with its fortunes for nearly twenty years. As contractor, he had built it, and worked it during its first few years of precarious existance ; he was one of the directors of the Rolling Stock Company, and was its chairman at the time of its dissolution. The closure of the line from 1872 to 1875 had released him from the onerous duty of working it, for when the line re-opened, the Receiver took over this responsibility. George Bush continued to further the interests of the railway as long as he had any connection with it, and can fairly be said to have been its longest and most faithful servant. He went into retirement in 1884, and was sadly missed by all his colleagues.

The Garstang & Knott-end Railway was now a going concern, and by 1896 its finances had undergone a complete transformation, thanks to the able guidance of the Receiver. It was now solvent, and capable of standing on its own feet, so the necessary steps to rid itself of the bonds of Chancery were taken, and the Receiver handed over officially to the directorate on 30th June 1897. The accounts for the first six months of that year showed that 302 first class and 19,715 third class passengers were carried, bringing in a revenue of £410 ; (if this seems a small amount for so many passengers, it must be remembered that the line was only seven miles in length, and by far the greater number were carried over the short section from the junction to Garstang Town, for which a third class fare of 3d. was charged.) On the goods side, 11,413 tons of general merchandise and 7,807 tons of minerals were carried, bringing in £1,529, plus £85 from miscellaneous items, including livestock. Against this was set £58 for the hire of " Hope ". With sundry odd items, the total revenue was £2,117, and expenditure £1,208, leaving a nett profit of £909 on the half-year's working.

On the 21st August 1897, making his annual address to the shareholders, the Chairman announced that a new engine had been purchased to replace " Hope ", though it was not yet in service, and it was hoped that the present state of prosperity continuing, there would be no further necessity to have to hire plant from outside.

The new engine, named "Jubilee Queen" in honour of Queen Victoria's diamond jubilee (which had taken place in 1897), was again a Hudswell Clarke 0-6-0 saddle tank, and a sister engine, "New Century" was purchased in 1900, these two replacing "Hope" and "Farmers Friend" respectively, both of which were taken in part exchange by the makers. The Garstang & Knott End Railway Engine Company, having outlived its usefulness, made its Return of Final Meeting on 12th October 1898, and was deemed, under the Companies Act, to have been dissolved on the expiration of three months from that date.

5. PROSPERITY

This new-found prosperity turned the thoughts of the directors to that part of the line which had never been built—the 4½ miles from Pilling to Knott End. Bearing in mind the vicissitudes of the early days, and as the company had only just got on its feet after thirty years in the "dog house", it was decided to float a separate company to build the extension. The original powers having long since lapsed anyway, it would be necessary to apply for new powers, and this might as well be done under a separate company. Accordingly, the Knott End Railway Company was incorporated on 12th August 1898, under Act of Parliament, with a nominal capital of £20,000, and naming three directors—Harry Chandos Elletson, Arthur William McNaghten, and Ernest Crosby—with a further two directors to be co-opted in due course. It was decided to do the work under direct labour, without the services of a contractor, and here again a bad mistake was made. Work commenced in 1900, and most of the roadbed had been made, along with the foundations of most of the buildings, when funds ran out, and the undertaking became moribund. The main cause of this debacle was the somewhat incomprehensible decision to divert the Knott End–Blackpool secondary road at the point where it crossed the railway at Preesall. Instead of a gated level crossing which sufficed for all other similar situations (including the main Lancaster–Blackpool road at Pilling) it was decided to raise the roadway 15 feet and build a plate girder overbridge on brick piers. This involved re-siting the road some twelve yards to the west, and constructing a long ramp at either end, on earth embankments, to carry the road. The resulting scheme was by far the most difficult engineering work on the whole line, and moreover, one that seemed to be totally unnecessary. It was this feature which ran away with the funds, and when work came to a standstill, the heavy brick abutments and earth embankments were barely completed, and the bridge remained uncompleted for almost eight years. £19,065 had been spent when it was decided to call a halt, leaving less than £1,000 capital still in hand.

The company applied for, and obtained, extensions of time for completion of the railway, but it began to look as if Knott End would never become the railhead. However, the United Alkali Co. projected a new works, with a salt mine, just south of Preesall, and this prospect of further remunerative traffic stimulated the Knott End Railway directorate to further efforts. A new prospectus was issued, and additional capital raised—somehow—to get the line finished. This time the work was let to a contractor (Worthington, of Dublin) on New Year's Day 1908, and so well did he get on with the job that it was completed by the middle of the following July, and opened for traffic on the 29th of that month. However, the Preesall overbridge was not completed, and the road diverted, until the following September, a temporary ungated level crossing being in use in the interim. All the remaining works were of a simple nature, the line being laid at ground level throughout, and virtually without gradients.

During the spring of 1908, a combined meeting of the two companies—the Garstang & Knot-end Railway, and the Knott End Railway—decided that the best way of getting over the difficulties entailed by two separate companies owning and working the two parts was by a merger. Hence it was arranged that the Knott End Railway should buy out the original company, lock, stock and barrel, for £50,000, the transaction to take effect from 1st July 1908. Parliamentary sanction for this was obtained under the Knott End Railway Act of 18th June. Thus the official ownership of the whole line from Garstang to Knott End was vested in the Knott End Railway Company, though it continued to use the old name of Garstang & Knott End Railway, even on some official documents, and lettered its rolling stock G. & K.E.R. This procedure was not, strictly speaking, correct, and has led to a great deal of confusion.

A further new locomotive was purchased for working the extended services, along with eight new coaches, six wagons and three brake vans. The engine was " Knott End ", an 0-6-0 side tank of somewhat larger dimensions than the previous stock, and was built by Manning Wardle & Co. of Leeds. The four original coaches of 1870 were by now in a very decrepit state, so they were withdrawn from service on the arrival of the new ones. These were of the "American" type (or at least that is how they were described in the press of that time), open saloons with end platforms, running on four-wheeled bogies. Four of them were third class only, and the other four were first and third composites. They were a vast improvement on the old six-wheeled coaches which had seen service from the beginning. As none of them had a guard's compartment, two passenger brake vans were bought to run with them, these being four-wheeled vehicles, without seating accommodation. The third brake van purchased at the same time was for goods service.

In the early part of 1908, before the merger of the two companies, the old G. & K.E.R. had bought two secondhand coaches from the Mersey Railway, but these were apparently never put into service. What happened to them is a mystery, since though their presence in the carriage shed at Garstang Town has been established (they were shown to the late T. R. Perkins on his official visit in 1908) they do not appear to have ever been used, and their ultimate fate is not known. They were apparently not in very good condition, for Perkins put it on record that the General Manager, who was showing him round, remarked that "they needed cleaning up a bit"—a masterpiece of understatement, according to Perkins. A further, and final, engine was added to stock in 1909, also a Manning Wardle product, named " Blackpool ". It was one of the very few 2-6-0 side tanks ever to work in this country, and was also the largest engine the company had. It was purchased mainly for goods traffic, but did a good share of hauling passenger trains as well. Both " Knott End " and " Blackpool " were fitted with the automatic vacuum brake when built, as were the eight new passenger coaches and the two brake vans of 1908; prior to this, no continuous brakes were ever used. The two earlier saddle tanks, " Jubilee Queen " and " New Century " did not have vacuum brakes when built, but were fitted in 1909 to bring them into line with the rest of the stock. Apart from the three brake vans, no goods stock was ever vacuum fitted. It would seem that these goods brake vans were vacuum fitted in 1908 before delivery of the two special passenger vans, so that they could work with the passenger stock. Though this was not necessary from the following year, the goods brakes retained their vacuum gear until sometime after the first World War, when it was removed from two of them, the third (No. 1) retained it throughout its life. Apart from six wagons purchased in 1912, there were no further additions to the rolling stock throughout the railway's independent existence.

Locomotive *Knott End* with one of the bogie saloons standing at Knott End Station.

Blackpool with both bogie saloons and four wheeled brake passenger coach.   *R. Kidner*

By the time that the Knott End extension had begun operations the total cost to the company had reached almost £230,000, this figure including the cost to the new company of the rolling stock delivered in 1908-9, and the purchase outright of the former Garstang & Knot-end Railway assets. £19,065 had been spent on the original Pilling–Knott End contract when work ceased, and the subsequent completion of the line and installations cost an additional sum of £44,690. The locomotive "Knott End", eight coaches, six wagons and three vans accounted for £110,000, while the purchase of the original Garstang–Pilling line, rolling stock, buildings and installations cost £50,000, as noted earlier. With £5,000 in shares, and £1,236 in legal and other charges, the total cost to the Knott End Railway Company was £229,991.

A new halt was opened at Carr Lane, half a mile to the west of Pilling in 1911, and a short branch, 1½ miles long, was laid to the newly-opened United Alkali Co.'s works near Preesall in 1912. This branch joined the main line in a trailing junction towards Knott End, so that all traffic to and from the works was marshalled in Knott End yard.

The passenger service in 1911, which was practically unaltered for the rest of the company's independent existence, allowed for three trains each way between Garstang and Catterall and Knott End, a morning train between the junction and Garstang Town only, and an evening train between Knott End and Garstang Town. A peculiar feature of this last train was shown by a special note in the 1908 timetable, that it would run through to Garstang and Catterall only if the total fares booked for this extra distance exceeded 3/-. Goods traffic was dealt with separately, by trains which ran as required between the passenger times. Pilling ceased to be a terminal point for any trains from 1908 onwards. In 1920, a steam rail motor was hired from the L.N.W.R., and this was still running on the line when the passenger service was discontinued in 1930.

The fortunes of the company can be judged from the amounts and value of the merchandise carried. In 1913, the first full year after the Preesall works were opened and were in full production, the railway carried 7,916 tons of salt from the works, and 13,663 tons of coal to them. In 1920, the figures had risen to 53,416 tons of salt and 24,135 tons of coal. Traffic in moss litter—used mainly for horse and cattle bedding—which was one of the main natural products of the district, was 2,117 tons in 1913, reaching its peak in 1916 with 6,854 tons, but a forced increase in cartage rates militated against this traffic, and it fell in 1917 to 4,727 tons, and by 1920 was but 2,600 tons. The rise in

GARSTANG AND KNOT-END RAILWAY

TIME TABLE for , 1870, and until further Notice.

NOTICE.

The published Time Tables of this Company are only intended to fix the time up to which Passengers may be certain to obtain their Tickets for a journey from the various Stations, it being understood the Trains do not start before the appointed time. Greenwich time will be kept. Every effort will be made to ensure punctuality, as far as practicable, but the Directors give distinct Notice, that the Company will not undertake that the Trains shall start or arrive at the exact time specified in the Bills; nor will they be accountable for any loss, inconvenience, or injury, which may arise from delays or detention in the starting, transit, or arrival of Trains. Passengers can only be conveyed from intermediate Stations when there is room in the Train.

UP		See Nos. 1	2	See Note 3	4	5	6	7	8	9	DOWN			10	11	12	13	14	15	See Nos. 16	17	16
Miles		a.m.	a.m.	a.m.	p.m.	p.m.	p.m.	p.m.	p.m.	p.m.	Miles			a.m.	a.m.	a.m.	p.m.	p.m.	p.m.	p.m.	p.m.	p.m.
0	Pilling Leave	7 10	....	10 17	....	4 0	....	....	....	....	0	Lancaster Leave		7 15	8 35	10 18	....	2 10	....	5 0	8 18	....
3	Winmarleigh ,,	7 20	....	10 27	....	4 12	....	....	....	....		Preston ,,		7 55	8 5	10 25	12 45	4 20	6 5	....	....	9 10
5	Garstang ,,	7 28	8 48	10 33	1 0	4 23	4 22	5 17	8 26	9 20		Garstang Junction (L.&N.W.) Arrive		8 30	9 4	10 54	1 12	2 40	4 45	6 25	8 41	9 34
7	Garstang Junction Arrive	7 35	8 55	10 42	1 7	2 32	4 31	5 24	3 59	9 27		Garstang Junction Depart		3 35	9 10	11 0	1 20	2 45	5 0	6 35	50 9	40
	Do. (L.&N.W.) Depart	7 45	9 4	10 50	1 12	2 40	4 45	5 32	8 41	9 34	2	Garstang ,,		8 42	9 16	11 7	1 27	2 52	5 7	6 42	56 9	46
	Preston Arrive	8 13	9 25	11 23	....	3 0	....	6 5	9 5	....	4	Winmarleigh ,,		9 24	....	....	....	3 0	....	6 50	....	....
	Lancaster ,,	8 55	....	11 25	1 48	....	5 20	6 53	....	10 5	7	Pilling Arrive		9 30	....	....	3 10	....	7 0	....	....

N.B. No. 3, on Thursday, this Train will leave Pilling at 9 40, and Winmarleigh at 9 50, arriving at Garstang at ten o'clock, in time for the Market.

Nos. 1 and 16. These Trains will not run between Pilling and Garstang Town, except on Thursdays and Saturdays.

☞ All the Trains will take up and set down Passengers at Cockerham Cross and Cogie Hill Crossing, when required.

All Trains First Class and Parliamentary. No Sunday Trains.

PASSENGER'S LUGGAGE.—Every Passenger travelling upon this Railway may take with him his ordinary Luggage, not exceeding 120 lbs. if a first class passenger, and 60 lbs. in weight if a third class passenger. Notice is however hereby given, that the Company will not be responsible for the care of the same, unless fully and properly addressed, with the name and destination of the party. not for any article conveyed inside the carriages.

CHILDREN under three years of age, free; those above three, and under twelve, half-price.

By Order,

John Noble Secretary

Offices, Garstang, Lancashire.

Wrightson, Printer and Stationer, Post Office, Garstang.

3 Copies sent the Board of Trade
November 16: 1870

The original timetable of 1870.

KNOTT END and GARSTANG.—Knott End.
General Manager, G. Erroll Worthington, Knott End.

Miles		Week Days.					Sundays.
		a	b	c	aft	aft	
	Knott End ....dep.	9 30	12 15	4	3 6	15	....
1½	Preesall	9 35	12 21	4	9 6	21	....
4	Pilling	7 46	9 45	12 31	4 19	6 31	....
7½	Nateby	Sig.	Sig.	Sig.	Sig.	Sig.	....
9	Garstang (430, 434)	8 3	10 0	12 48	4 36	6 45	....
11	Garstang & Catterall arr.	8 11	10 7	12 6	4 44		....

Miles		Week Days.					Sundays.
			mrn	c	mrn	b	a
	Garstang & Catterall dp.		8 32	10 32	1 15	5 10	....
2	Garstang	Saturdays only	7 58	8 42	10 42	1 25	5 20	....
4	Nateby		Sig.	8 49	Sig.	Sig.	Sig.	....
7	Pilling		7 30	8 59	10 59	1 42	5 37	....
10	Preesall		....	9 3	11 3	1 52	5 47	....
11½	Knott End arr.		....	9 13	11 13	1 56	5 51	....

a Calls at Cogie Hill and Cockerham Cross on Saturdays when required. **b** Calls at Cogie Hill and Cockerham Cross on Thursdays and Saturdays when required. **c** Calls at Cogie Hill and Cockerham Cross on Fridays when required. **s** Saturdays only.

Bradshaw's timetable of 1911.

GARSTANG AND CATTERALL AND KNOTT END (KNOTT END RAILWAY).

	Week days.						Week days.				
		C		A	B				B		A	C	
	a.m.	a.m.	a.m.	p.m.	p.m.			a.m.	a.m.	p.m.	p.m.	
Lancaster ....depart	7 50	9 48	....	1 0	4 40	....	Knott End ....depart	....	9 25	12 20	4 0	6 10
Preston .... ,,	7 55	10 10	....	12 50	4 30	6 40	Preesall	....	9 29	12 24	4 4	6 14
Garstang & Catterall ..depart	8 25	....	10 28	1 33	5 13	....	Pilling	7S47	9 40	12 35	4 15	6 25
Garstang	8 31	....	10 S	1 39	5 19	....	Nateby	....	....	....	....	....
Nateby	8 40	....	....	....	....	....	Garstang	....	9 57	12 52	4 32	6 42
Pilling	8 50	....	11 3	1 58	5 38	....	Garstang & Catterall arrive	8 8	10 8	1 1	4 42	6 52
Preesall	9 2	....	11 15	2 10	5 50	....	Preston .... arrive	8 37	10 45	2 0	5 37	7 25
Knott End ....arrive	9 7	....	11 20	2 15	5 55	....	Lancaster	8 55	11 3	1 47	5 24	7 38

A—Calls at Cogie Hill, Cockerham Cross, and Carr Lane on Thursdays and Saturdays when required.
B—Calls at Cogie Hill, Cockerham Cross, and Carr Lane on Saturdays when required.
C—Calls at Cogie Hill, Cockerham Cross, and Carr Lane on Fridays when required.
S—Saturdays only.

All trains will call at Nateby and Carr Lane when required to set down on notice being given to the guard at the previous station or to pick up if notice be given to the Station Master at Nateby.

LNWR timetable of 1921.

motor traffic towards the end of the first World War showed its effect on the transport of cask beer, which in 1913 practically all went by rail, to the tune of 356 tons ; in 1920 this had fallen to the ridiculous figure of one ton !

6. DECLINE AND FALL

The Grouping of Railways Act of 1919–20 gave the Knott End line to the London, Midland & Scottish Railway, and it then became merely an unimportant branch of a large company. In 1922, the proposals of the L.M.S.R. for take-over were negotiated, these being that holders of £50,000 of K.E. debenture stock should receive an equal amount of L.M.S. 3% preference shares. The K.E. ordinary shares should be cancelled, and arrears of interest on K.E. debentures should also be cancelled. These terms were not acceptable to the Knott End shareholders, but in the ultimate settlement of 1923, the terms were even less favourable, and the Knott End shareholders had to be content with 125/- of L.M.S. ordinary stock for every £100 of K.E. ordinary, debenture holders to receive an equal amount of L.M.S. debentures at par.

Compared with 1913, the last complete year of Knott End accounts (1922) showed a satisfactory increase, though the total of passengers fell from 91,918 in 1913 to 77,579 in 1922; 69,535 tons of goods were carried in the latter year, against 19,043 tons in 1913 ; total revenue increased from £5,973 to £12,815, and expenditure from £4,794 to £11,583. The 1922 accounts showed a nett profit of £1,232 on the year's working, compared with £1,179 in 1913.

Though the line had apparently a good period of prosperity, and was in a sound financial position, this was unhappily not to continue. The L.M.S.R. re-organised the timetable in 1924, to give six trains each way daily (except Sundays) between Garstang and Catterall and Knott End ; one morning train from Garstang Town to Knott End, and a corresponding return train in the evening which ran through to the junction if required ; also two trains each way between the junction and Garstang Town only. The first train from Garstang Town to the terminus and from Knott End to Garstang and Catterall, as well as one in the afternoon, were first and third class, the remainder being third class only.

The majority of these services were dealt with by the rail motor. Seating 48 third class passengers, this vehicle originally operated in L.N.W.R. colours, but was later repainted in L.M.S. red with the number 10698. However, the rapid growth of road transport in the late 'twenties made the passenger service unremunerative, and it was entirely withdrawn on and from 31st March, 1930, the last trains running on Saturday, 29th March, as there was no Sunday service. Branch line closures in those days were not the widely publicised affairs that they are today. But fortunately the late J. E. N. Ashworth chose to visit the railway for this occasion, and afterwards recorded his trip in the *Railway Magazine*. Starting from Knott End, he bought the last return ticket over the whole length of the line. The crew of the railmotor, which for the final year operated a reduced passenger service alone, were on their last trip. The journey was notable for the people joining the train at the stops, some taking their children for last rides. At Garstang Town most of these left, along with that train crew. Having been down to the junction the railmotor returned for the final westerly journey, and, again crowded, it proceeded with an accompaniment of whistling and fog signals to Knott End, the crossing-keepers and local inhabitants gathering at the crossing to wave and watch it pass. Mr. Ashworth waited as the final train rounded the curve from the terminus in a cloud of steam, and last heard it as it arrived at Preesall amid whistling and detonator bangs.

At the end the service consisted of five trains a day each way, weekdays only, with two extra each way between Garstang Town and the junction only. The average time taken for the $11\frac{1}{2}$ miles was 38 minutes. The replacing 'bus service consisted of six trips one way and seven the other. The stations remained open for parcels and goods, but the halts were completely closed. The freight traffic was then worked by ex-Lancashire & Yorkshire Railway Barton Wright 0-6-2 tanks, two of which, Nos. 11613/6 were in Garstang shed on the final day. Other common performers of this class at times between 1928 and 1930 were Nos. 11604/12/7/8, and Webb 4' 3" 0-6-2T (still bearing L.N.W.R. No. 780) also appeared. After Garstang Town shed closed the line was worked from Preston depot with a variety of motive power : L. & Y.R. 0-6-0, L.N.W.R. " Cauliflower " 0-6-0, L.N.W.R. 0-8-0, B.R. Class 2 2-6-0's of the 78000 series, and L.M.S. Class Fives.

In 1925, just five years before the passenger service terminated, a dispute arose with the United Alkali Co. over cartage rates which caused that concern to install a pipe line under the River Wyre to their older works at Burn Naze, on the outskirts of Fleetwood, and to start pumping brine to the other side for processing. Except for maintaining the pumping plant and mine, the Preesall works were shut

Class 5 No. 44764, 4–6–0 at Garstang Town Station on the 14th June 1963 having just taken on water.
M.R. Price

The remains of Nateby Station in 1963.
M.R. Price

down, and some very lucrative traffic was lost to the railway. However, it seems that the mineral branch remained until about 1934, when it was lifted and the last locomotives, which can have had precious little to do in the intervening years, were disposed of. About this time also the moss litter works near Cogie Hill crossing, once apparently sponsored by Dutch interests, closed as well, and more traffic was lost.

Road competition continued to increase, but the Knott End line was still occasionally used for passenger excursions. The passage of time has confused details of these trains, but there seems to be little doubt that they did function, often with main line stock and locomotives. Some are said to have run to Scotland, and even to Dunstable (for Whipsnade Zoo), having travelled the whole of the G. and K.E. route calling at each of the stations. It is certain, however, that these ceased with the start of the Second World War, although the goods traffic, which had dwindled in the 'thirties, received a short respite during the hostilities.

The war was notable in other ways for the Knott End line. During Royal tours of the North, Garstang Town was twice, on 28th August 1940, and 30th October, 1941, used as an overnight stabling point for the Royal Train. North of Garstang and Catterall, where the railway ran parallel with the L.M.S. main line, the laying in of connections between the two converted the former into a down main line goods loop, this being operational from 20th September, 1942. About this time also a corresponding up goods refuge was put in.

By 1947 the service was down to one daily pick-up goods between Garstang and Catterall and Knott End. On 13th November, 1950, after just 42 years of use, the section from Pilling to Knott End closed completely, whilst Nateby was shut down altogether. Track lifting west of Pilling started in the spring of 1951, and when this work was completed arrangements were made for the sale of the land. One local story, which doubtless should be treated with some reserve, has it that the copper wire used with the telegraph posts was accidentally left in place so that, having disposed of the land, the railway authorities found they had to buy back the wire. The price demanded (so the story goes !) was almost equivalent to that gained for the ground, and thus the total profit was negligible ! In the course of the dismantling the awkwardly situated crossing at Pilling was taken out ; the gates lay rotting in the grass nearby for some years after. At Preesall all the buildings except for the goods shed were swept away ; now only part of a platform remains, by which an agricultural depot has recently been established. The girder bridge over the route at this point was bricked in. After the closure of the Knott End extension, furthermore, the line was operated on the one-engine-in-steam principle, a staff being carried on the daily goods to unlock the keys on the points, as at Pilling. Upper-quadrant " fixed " distants were installed six hundred yards from each crossing, and the stations were similarly protected.

On 1st May, 1954, during a railtour by the Stephenson Locomotive and Manchester Locomotive Societies, the special train ran to Pilling behind ex-L.M.S. Fowler Class 4 2-6-4T No. 42316. Difficulty was then encountered in running the engine round the train, owing to the shortness of the loop in the goods yard—this point having been used as the terminus because of the crumbling platform edges. Eventually the problem was resolved by dividing the modern carriage stock.

The only remaining regular working on the railway was then, of course, the " Pilling Pig ". Under the 1962-63 winter timetables it functioned weekdays only as follows:

Preston (North Union Yard) ...	dep.	11.24 a.m.
Garstang and Catterall	dep.	12.45 p.m.
Pilling	arr.	2.05 p.m.
Pilling	dep.	2.45 p.m.
Garstang and Catterall	arr.	3.53 p.m.
Preston (North Union Yard) ...	arr.	6.08 p.m.

The train crew came from Preston, although a porter usually travelled up to Pilling from Garstang and Catterall also. The locomotive, then almost invariably a Class 5 4-6-0, might be from some quite foreign depot, as both immediately before and after the Pilling duty it was employed on passenger workings. The train was marshalled in North Union Yard (to the south-west of the passenger station) by a diesel shunter, and then handed over to the Class 5. It had no scheduled stops on the main line until Garstang and Catterall was reached, but once there might spend a considerable time shunting only a few wagons because of the awkward layout of the goods yard. The chief traffic to this point was paper pulp, this having been brought into Preston Dock from abroad, loaded into wagons, and propelled up to North Union Yard to join the train. From Garstang and Catterall is was taken to one of the oldest paper mills in Lancashire, at Oakenclough, for processing, and then returned to a new factory by the Station for making up into paper towels. *

*These are boxed and loaded into vans ready to be picked up by the freight on its return from Pilling.

Close to Garstang and Catterall station and parallel with the main line a new by-pass for Garstang is, at the time of writing, under construction. This is due to give the railway fresh traffic, for it is anticipated that from April 1964 large quantities of gravel will be required each day for the work. For convenience in unloading, Garstang Town is to be used rather than Garstang and Catterall, and this means that the loop round the back of the island platform at the former station will have to be linked up again in order to accommodate the wagons. Latterly the principal traffic to Garstang Town and to Pilling was in coal. A great variety of other goods might be taken, but were normally of an agricultural nature ranging from seed potatoes to cattle foodstuffs. Livestock traffic was virtually dead, and it was very seldom that more than three or four wagons were taken right through to Pilling.

The start of the 1963 summer timetables also saw the retirement of the last two permanent way maintenance men on the Knott End line. Between them they had over eighty years of service to their credit! The track was then cared for by a squad of travelling gangers responsible for several branch lines in the north-west.

On 31st July, 1963, the anticipated closure of the Garstang Town–Pilling section took place, and the last " Pilling Pig " that day was handled by Class 5 No. 45390.

7. THE LINE DESCRIBED

Originally the line was laid with 48 lb./yd. iron rails (in all probability secondhand) fastened to longitudinal sleepers with coach screws. One portion was, however, 56 lb./yd. rail of bridge section, but likewise set in ash ballast. It was not until the better days of the late 1880's that any improvement was made, transverse sleepering and 88 lb./yd. steel rails being gradually introduced according to the resources of the company. There are still one or two sections of track in existence dating back to the turn of the century, and as this equipment appears to be of L.N.W.R. origin it seems possible that the G. & K.E. got at least some of its supplies from Crewe. The Knott End extension was also laid with 88 lb./yd. rail, mainly in chairs, but some flat-bottomed rail was used latterly, probably as replacement. The ash ballast was universal until fairly recent times. Maintenance on the whole was very good—after the 1872 debacle—the track being kept free from weeds, although in L.M.S. days this was not the case.

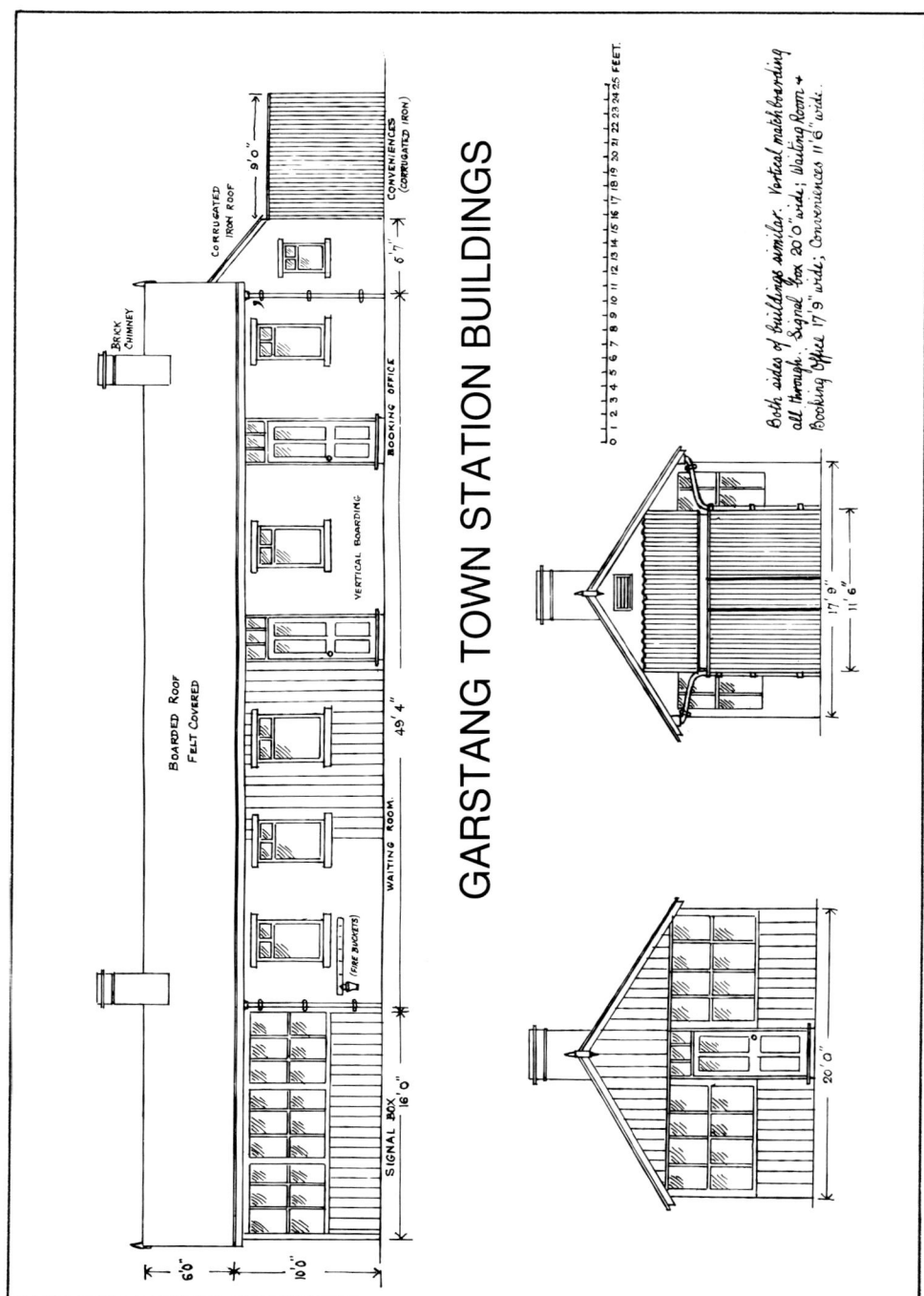

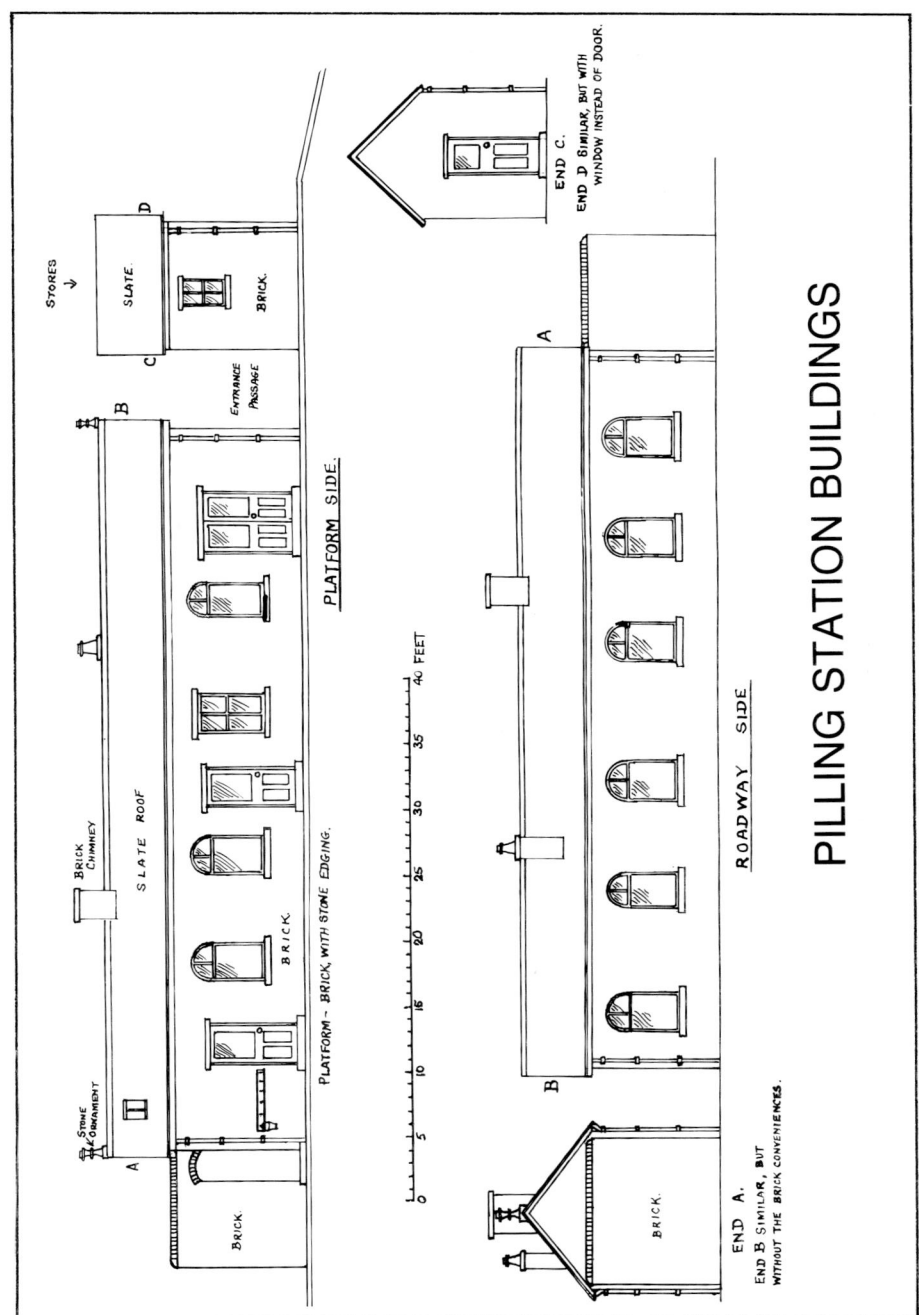

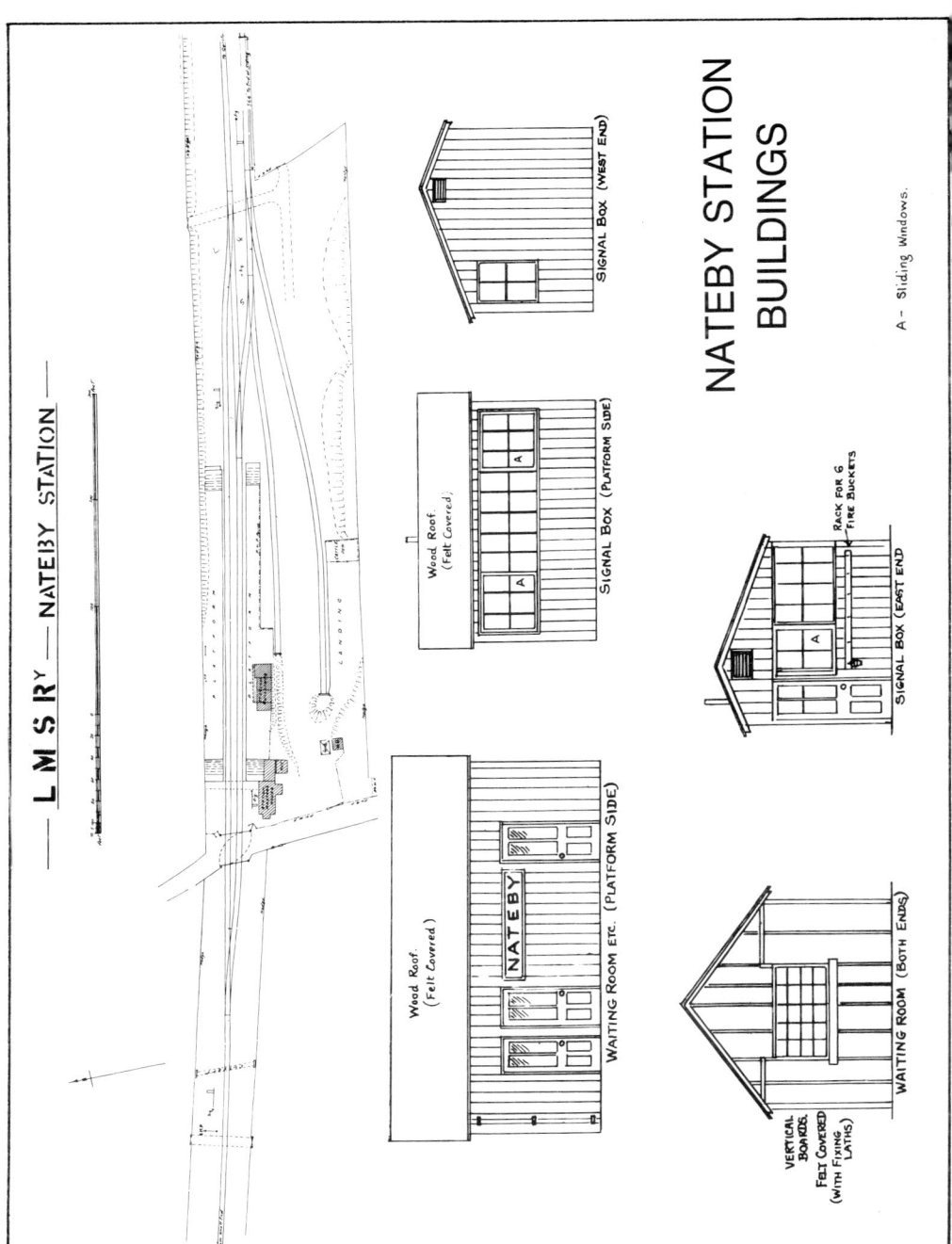

PREESALL STATION BUILDINGS

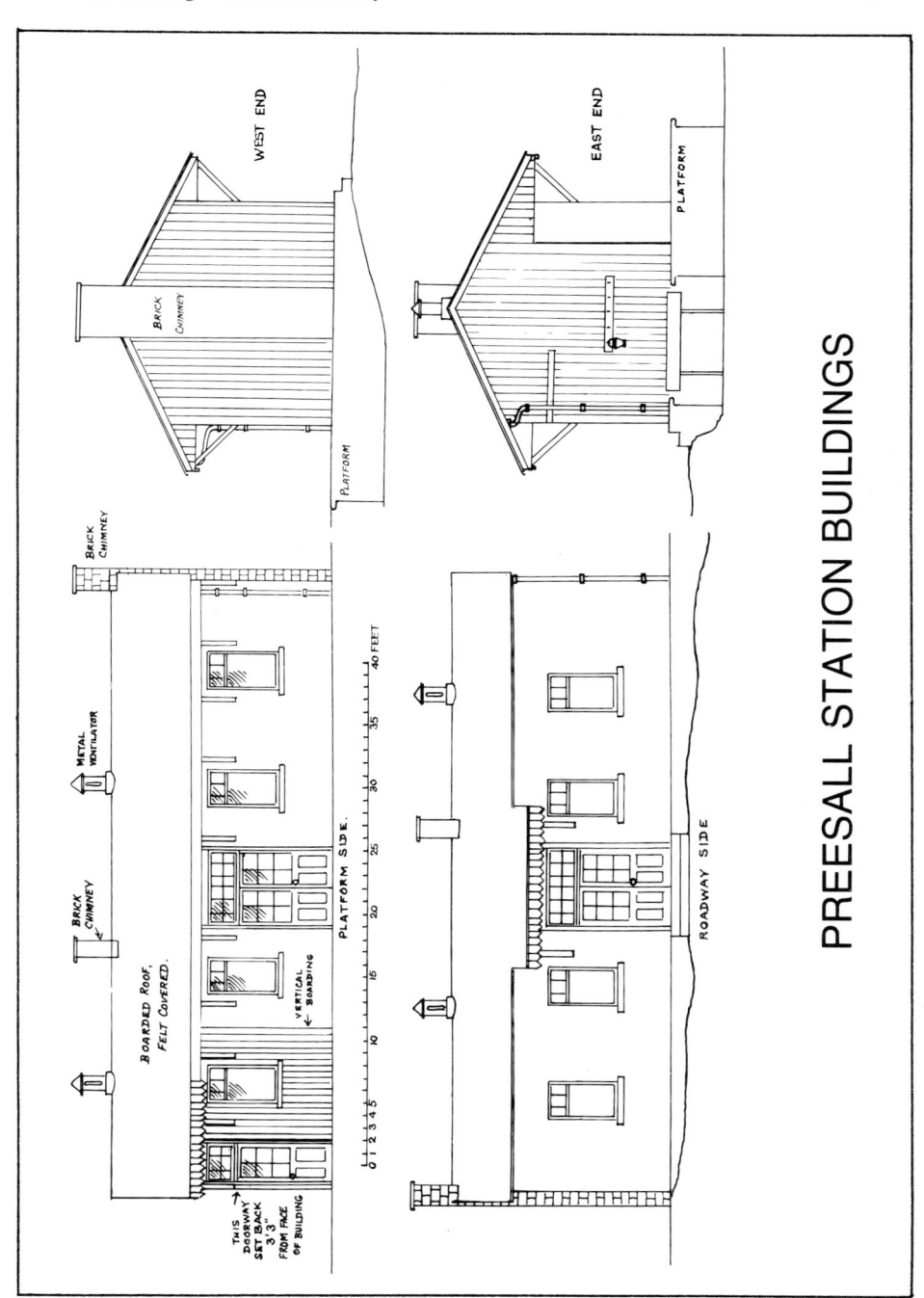

GARSTANG TOWN

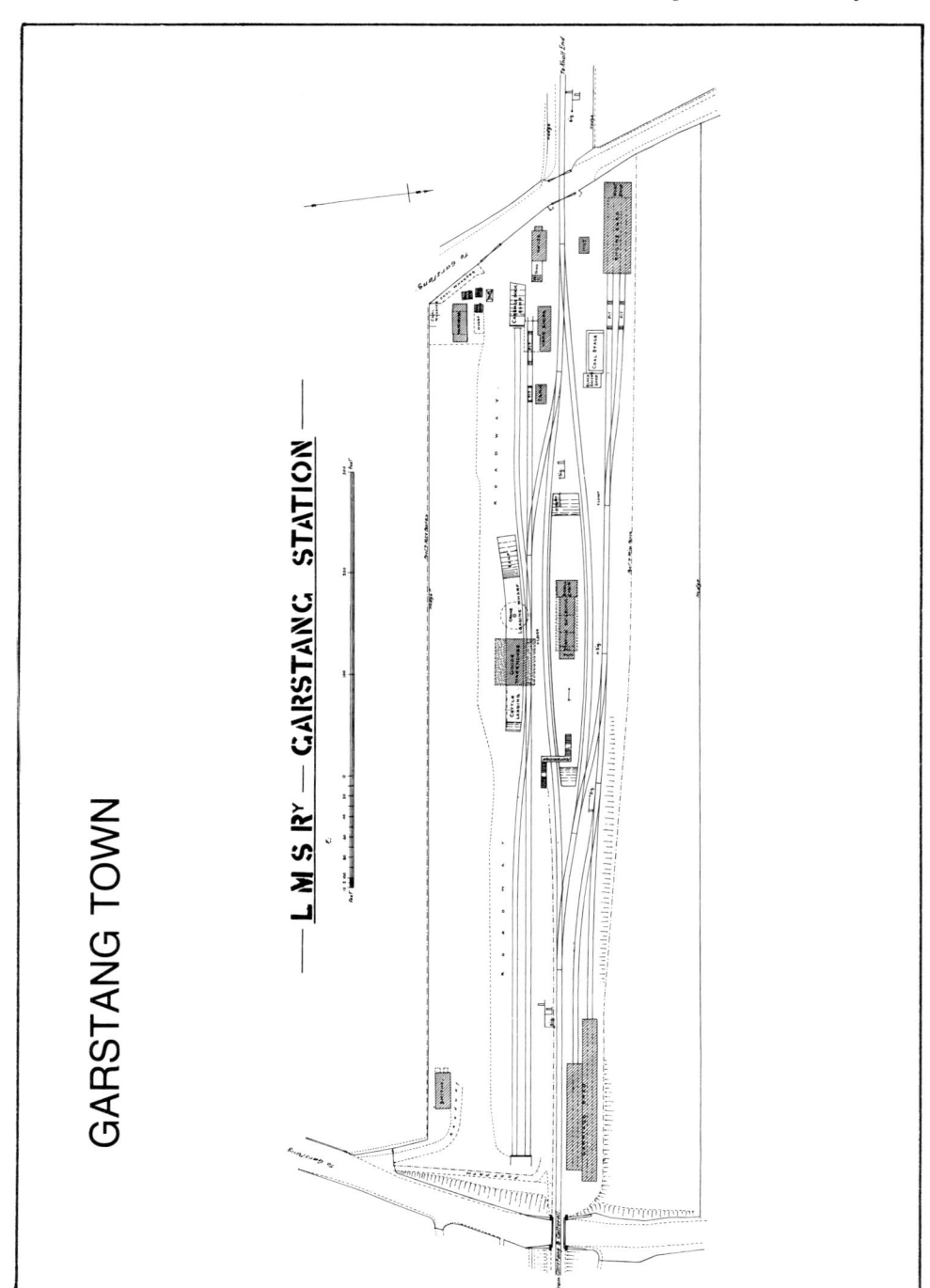

— L M S RY — GARSTANG STATION —

The Garstang & Knott End Railway 35

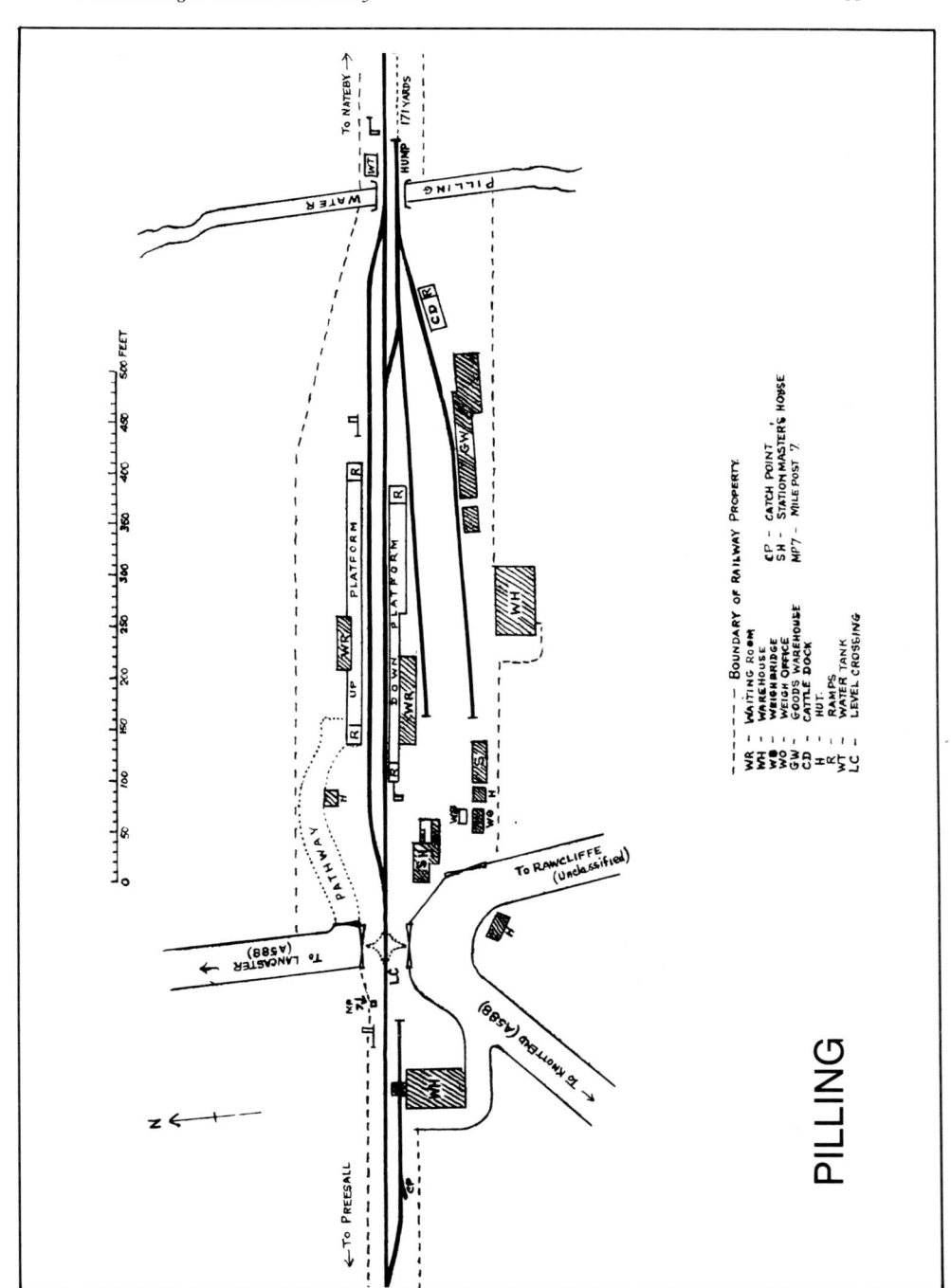

PILLING

L.M.S.RY — PREESALL STATION

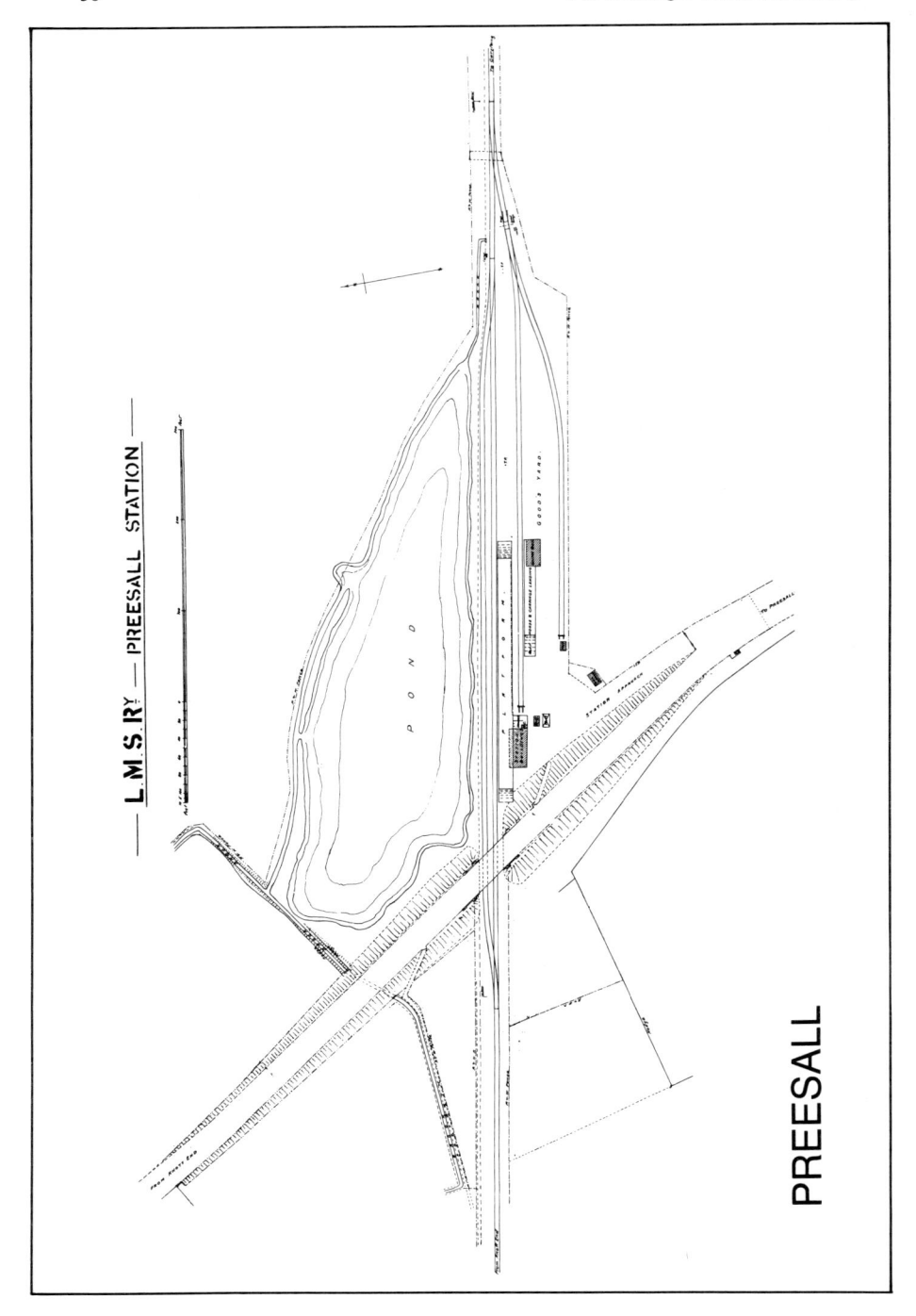

PREESALL

— L.M.S.RY — KNOTT-END STATION —

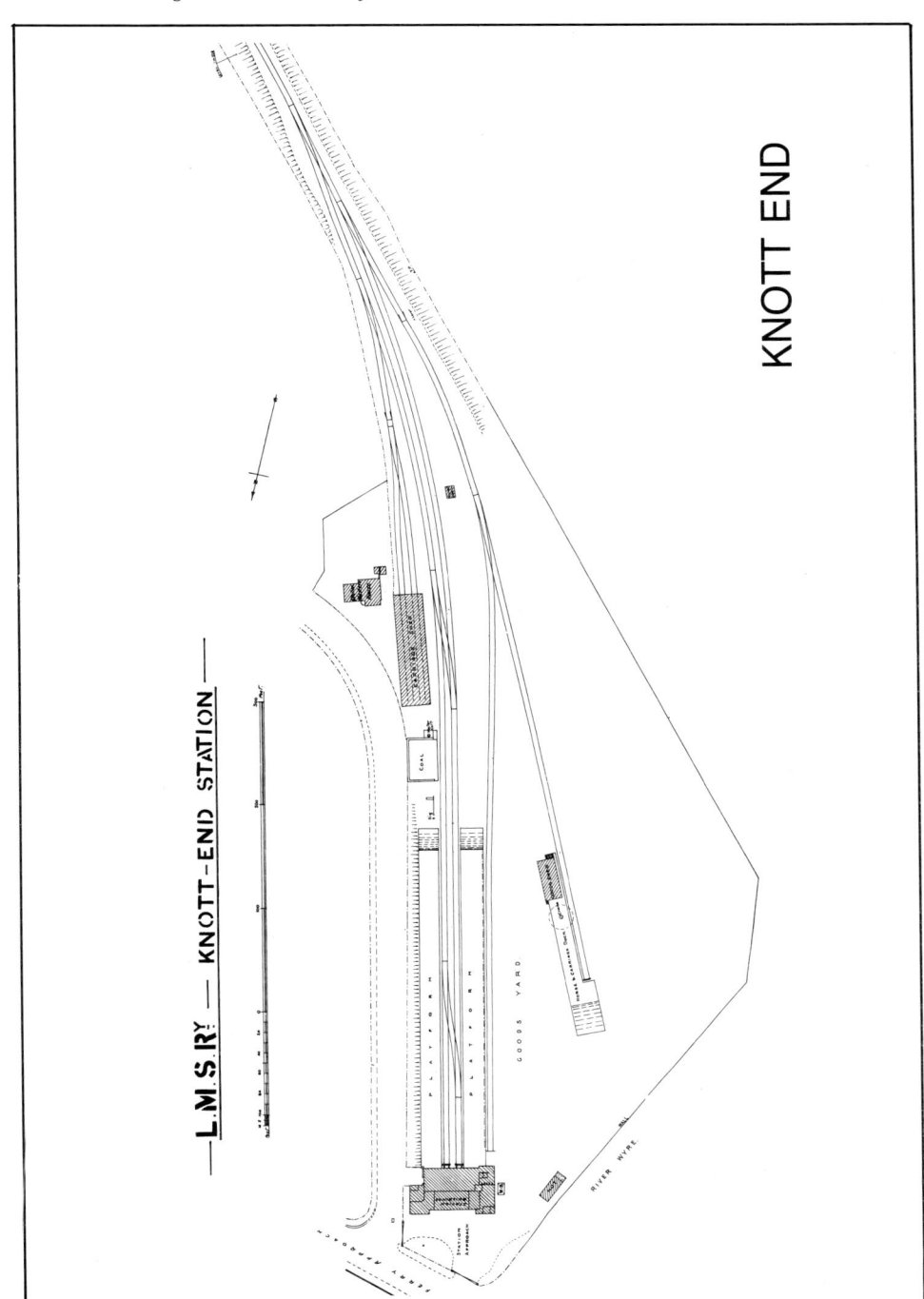

KNOTT END

GARSTANG & CATTERALL STATION

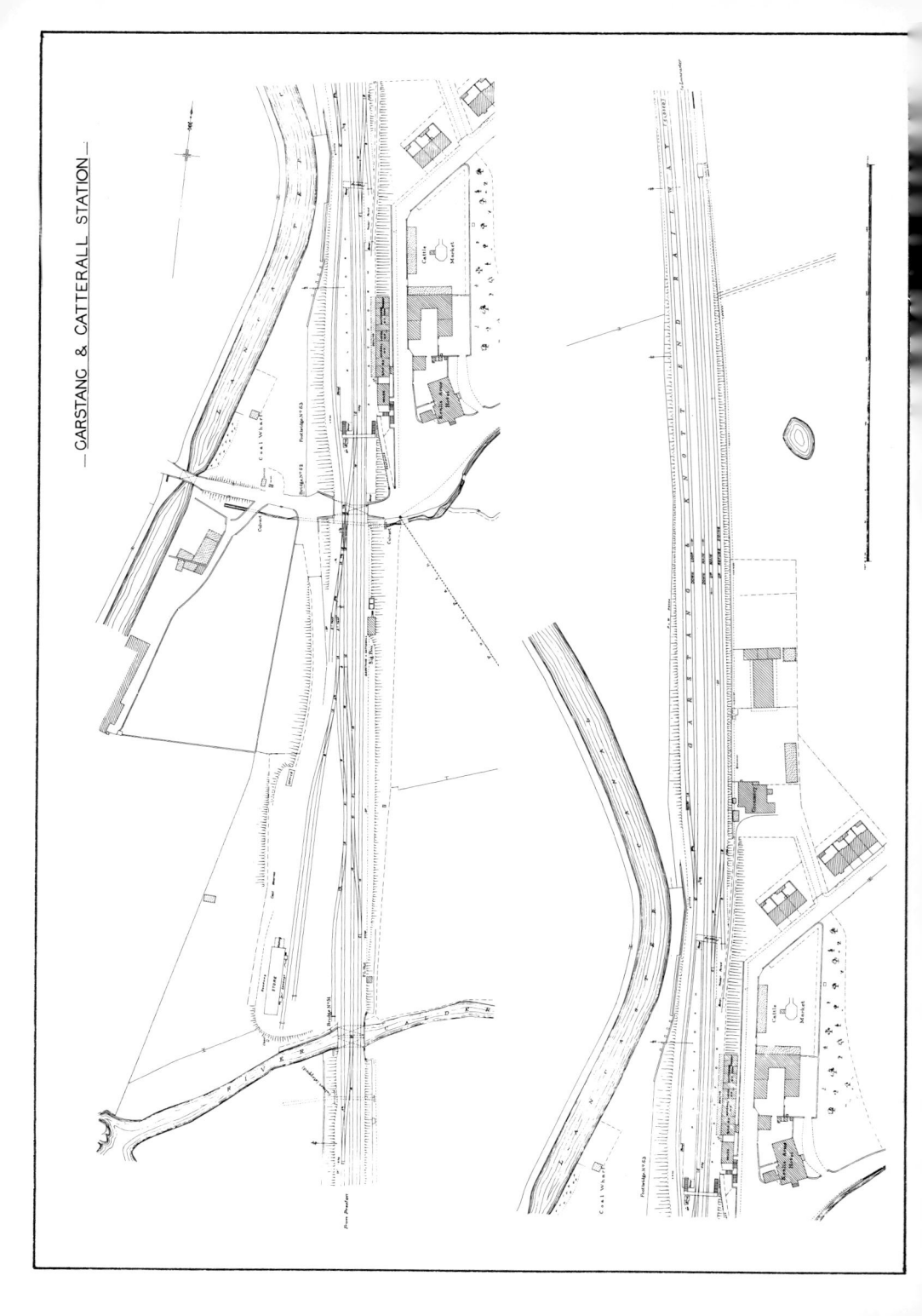

In the beginning, the directors did have the foresight to purchase enough land for double track (about the only foresight they ever had) as this was comparatively cheap. Similarly the bridges were built on the assumption that one day there might be two tracks, but as it transpired even in the busy and prosperous days about the time of the First World War, the double line was never laid. The unused ground was by no means a dead loss, however, for the company cultivated it with meadow grass. At suitable intervals it was cut by railway workers, loaded into a truck and conveyed to Nateby station where it was built up into a haystack prior to sale to the local farmers for hay. T. R. Perkins, in his 1908 *Railway Magazine* article, recorded that on the occasion of his visit the train was delayed at Nateby briefly whilst the empty hay truck was manipulated into a siding—the kind of unusual incident that is peculiar to the rural railway. In later years, much of the spare ground between Pilling and Knott End was let off as allotments to railwaymen and local residents at a nominal rent.

The line began at Garstang and Catterall station, on the L.N.W.R. main line, some 11 miles north of Preston. The only direct connection with the L.N.W.R. was in the goods yard, a short distance south of the station, whence the line ran along the outer face of the down platform, which was an island. A short loop opposite the signal box provided the run-round facilities for Knott End trains. The up platform contained the main station buildings, which were very substantial, and occupying a space of some 125 feet by 20 feet. The whole station was built on an embankment, and from the roadway below presented a rather gloomy and forbidding appearance, the buildings being supported on nine brick arches on the outside, and a larger arch under each end wall. The hipped roof was of slate, with considerably overhanging eaves, the guttering supported on stone giving a somewhat ornate appearance to the roofing. Windows were all round topped, and arranged in groups of three, though the fourth and sixth groups had only two. The main building was divided into eight sections, in this order, starting from the southern end: Stationmaster's Office; Booking Office; General Waiting Room; Ladies' Room; First Class Waiting Room; Porters' Room; Stores; Gents' Conveniences. On the platform side was a glass awning running the whole length of the building. There was no direct access from the roadway to the station buildings; a sloping path ran up the side of the embankment from the corner by the bridge to the platform, and there were also two flights of steps from the roadway behind the main buildings. The upper flight was of wood, but the

Garstang and Catterall goods yard and signal box taken on the 14th June 1963. *M.R. Price*

A general view of Garstang and Catterall Station taken on the 14th June 1963. *M.R. Price*

An LMS steam Railmotor No. 10698 at Garstang and Catterall main line station seen here before its last run to Knott End station on the 29th April 1930. The train behind is the 4.15 p.m., Morecambe (Euston Road) to Preston, hauled by Prince Class 4–6–0. The water in the foreground is the Preston–Lancaster Canal. *J.N. Ashworth*

D234 diesel hauling the up "Caledonian" express seen here passing through Garstang and Catterall Station on the 14th June 1963. *M.R. Price*

Garstang Town Station in 1930 showing the unique footbridge and station buildings.
LGRP. Courtesy David & Charles

Locomotive *New Century* standing on a train at Garstang. *M.R. Price*

lower flight was of stone, running between brick walls and split into two parts running in opposite directions.

Separated from the main buildings at the south end by a gap of about eight feet, was the stationmaster's house. This most peculiar building had apparently no chimneys, and the occupants went downstairs to bed, since the living room and door were on platform level, and the other rooms beneath. There was no access from the street. At one time, as the extensive buildings imply, this was a very busy station, but at the present day there are only two trains which call there each day in each direction, and the gate is kept locked for the greater part of the day.

So far, the architecture is purely L.N.W.R., but the down island platform was different. There were formerly two wooden buildings here, the larger a purely L.N.W.R. affair combining waiting room and stores. Separated by a short space was a small, doll's house sort of structure which was the G. & K.E.R. booking office, constructed later to a similar design. This booking office has now entirely disappeared, and as the L.N.W.R. building is now in a ruinous condition, without roof, one is unable to get much idea of the original appearance, beyond the fact that the boarding was horizontal. It is said that originally both sides of this building were alike, but at the present, the K.E. side presents a blank face. Opposite the station was a large hotel, the Kenlis Arms, adjoining the cattle market, and these were built of the same dark brick as the station. Further along the road were a few small cottages and a dairy. The bridge at the end of the station was rather interesting. Originally it was built to carry only two tracks—the L.N.W.R. main line—and was a solid stone structure with a semi-circular arch, giving a road clearance of 11' 6", and a width of only ten feet. When the G. & K.E. track was added, the necessary widening was carried out by extending the abutments and putting a plate girder across on the western side, with a steel deck. This part had a road clearance of 12' 6". The widening of the bridge was the responsibility of the G. & K.E.R., and was at their expense.

Leaving the north end of the platform, the line, now single, ran alongside the L.N.W.R. at a slightly lower level, for about half a mile, and was crossed by two stone overbridges, which also spanned the L.N.W.R. tracks. Turning rather sharply westwards, the Knott End track passed under a third bridge and a wooden footbridge; apart from the Blackpool Road bridge at Preesall, these were the only overbridges on the line until 1928, when the new Garstang bypass road

Early postcard view of Nateby Station in 1906.

A crude but effective distant signal near Nateby.

Haymaking off the side of the track near Nateby in July 1906.

Courtesy Railway Magazine

was constructed, which necessitated building a further overbridge ; this however, was not the responsibility of the railway. Almost immediately after passing under the wooden footbridge, the River Wyre was crossed on a plate girder bridge, and the first gradient of note began here, a rise of 1 in 125 for one mile, to the precincts of Garstang Town station, the road at the eastern end of the yard being crossed by another plate girder bridge. From here onwards, all other roads were crossed on the level. At Garstang Town was the headquarters of the company, with offices, engine and carriage sheds, and a small workshop for dealing with light repairs, the whole being situated at the northern end of the town. With the exception of the office buildings and the goods warehouse, which were of brick, the bulk of the construction was wood and corrugated iron. Entering the station yard from the east, on the right were the carriage sheds, a long, low building of wood, with liberal patches of corrugated iron. The line immediately divided into two, passing round both sides of a single island platform, both faces of which were continuous curves, and joined up again just before reaching the level crossing at the other end of the yard. A branch off the up platform line led directly to the two-road engine shed, with its workshop at the rear, each road having an inspection pit outside the shed. Adjoining was a large coal bin. From the down platform road, a line led to the goods warehouse, with a crane, cattle dock, and two sidings. This warehouse was of brick, whitewashed. By the level crossing was another brick building which housed the company's offices, and close by was another small workshop and a water tank. The blacksmith's shop was located far away from the rest, opposite the carriage sheds, and has, for many years past, been the permanent way ganger's cabin.

From the passenger point of view, the station, though in a convenient situation at the north of the town, was extremely inconveniently laid out. Access to the platforms could only be obtained by crossing the whole of the goods yard, and the main line. An iron footbridge, with reversed ends, was built for this purpose, but was not greatly used, passengers preferring to cross the lines at ground level. The station was one of those things which are always scheduled for improvements, but somehow never get done—quite a common occurrence in railway circles ! The buildings were quite unpretentious ; wood construction with corrugated iron here and there was the rule. There was merely a booking office and a waiting room. The present buildings were put up in about 1911, replacing the original structure which Perkins described in his 1908 article as being " a tiny brick building, roofed with

Pilling Station on the 1st May 1954 with an Enthusiasts Special having just arrived. This view shows both platforms and signal box. *R. Kidner*

Pilling Station with the new signal box and station facilities under construction. *R. Kidner*

Pilling Station level crossing. *R. Kidner*

galvanised iron, and devoid of all pretensions to convenience". To judge from an illustration in the 1908 1d. Guide to the railway this description is most apt ; it is not easy to tell, however, exactly where it was located, although it would appear to have been on the south side of the line somewhere near the present goods warehouse.

The most astonishing feature of the " new " station was its signal box, for this remarkable edifice—in the usual wood and iron—abutted directly on to the main station buildings. It was glazed on three sides, and its vastness could have housed the lever frame of a typical main line junction, let alone the meagre equipment of Garstang Town. To what use it was put besides the signalling installation is something of a mystery. A gravel roadway ran through the length of the yard, the approach at the eastern end, near the overbridge being rather steep, since the main road at this point was at a considerably lower level.

Today Garstang Town possesses a depressing air which even the daily arrival of the " Pilling Pig " does little to dispel. The extensive station building and signalbox virtually bereft of paint, not having been so treated since November, 1926. The old carriage sheds have lately decayed considerably, although the locomotive shed is rather better as it is still in use as an agricultural store. Across the road to the west of the station one of the American-style coach bodies, stripped of all fittings, survives as a sizeable hen-house. The rails into the locomotive and carriage sheds have been lifted, and the rest of the track on the up side is overgrown and rusty : the up track into the island platform has been disconnected at the west end.

Leaving the station a gated level crossing took the line over a secondary road, and thence falling at 1 in 188 for approximately a mile, it passed beneath the by-pass overbridge to reach the Lancaster Canal. The present plate girder bridge is the third in that place, the original wooden bridge being rebuilt in 1908, and the present one being erected by the L.M.S.R. From the canal there was a short level stretch, followed by a descent of 1,600 yards at 1 in 73—the only real " bank " on the whole line—through a shallow cutting. Thence the route curved on a short embankment (along this stretch quite a sizeable section of dilapidated 1901 track survived until closure : preparations to relay it were abandoned when the line came under threat of shut-down).

Near the end of the embankment was Nateby station, which had a passing loop and two sidings. (All these have been dismantled for some number of years ; the present single running line is on the site of the original loop.) This station was originally named Winmarleigh, from

Preesall Station just after opening, showing the station buildings and road crossing gates underneath the new road bridge. *R. Kidner*

The new station from the road bridge at Preesall with locomotive *Knott End* on a train of two new bogie saloons and brake van. *R. Kidner*

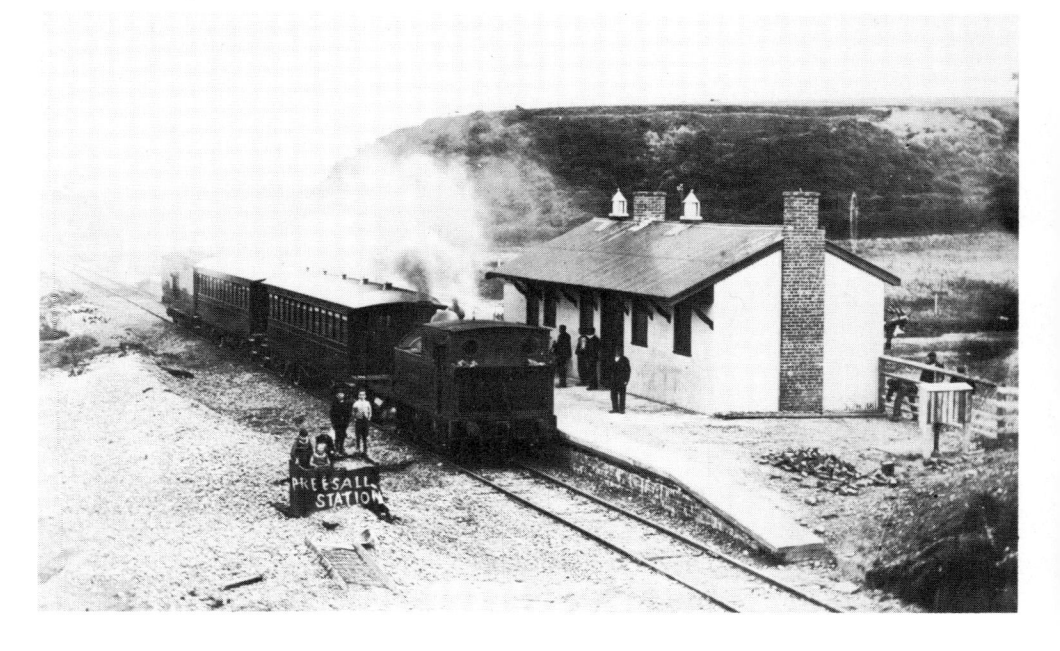

the neighbouring estate of that name, but was changed in 1906 in order to eliminate confusion with the village of Winmarleigh, which was some five miles away to the north. The station being just outside the village of Nateby, this name was more appropriate. In the old days, there was a small wooden building on the single platform, and a crossing keeper's cottage of brick beside the level crossing at the west end of the station. Subsequently—as near as can be ascertained—about 1902, the building was replaced by a smaller one in the usual corrugated iron decor, this abutting on to a signal box of similar " greenhouse " pattern to the one at Garstang, except that it was only glazed on two sides. This signal box and the cottage are all that remain now. The crossing loop had been taken out by 1908, though the sidings remained several years longer ; their chief use was for the hay traffic which was mentioned in an earlier chapter; it will be remembered that the hay cut from the spare land along the line was taken to Nateby for stacking and subsequent sale.

Continuing in a dead straight line, and practically level on the surface of the land, Pilling was reached, three miles beyond Nateby, and seven miles from the junction. In between were two "halts", named Cogie Hill and Cockerham Crossing, both being situated where the line crossed secondary roads. There is some controversy as to whether these ever had platforms, although the 1908 1d. Guide and other authorities are positive in stating that there were small erections used as stopping places on market days only. Cogie Hill evidently did once possess a short hump of ashes, however, for this purpose, until it was flattened by use. In addition there were small signboards, although Cogie Hill situated on the slightest undulation of the ground could not, by any stretch of the imagination, be called a hill. This crossing is the only one of the two to retain proper gates, and there is now little trace of the Moss Litter Works which once stood nearby.

Pilling was the terminus of the line from 1870 until 1908, and reverted to that status in 1950. (Incidentally, Pilling station is actually in the village of Stakepool, about a mile away from the real village of Pilling.) As befits a terminus, its layout and buildings were rather more pretentious. Moreover, it possessed the only " hump " shunting neck on the whole line. Approaching from Nateby, the shunting neck, 171 yards long, was at a slightly higher level on the south side, rising to the summit of the hump immediately before the bridge which crossed a small stream known as Pilling Water. Beside the main line on the bank of the stream was a water tank, conveniently situated for drawing

A fine period photograph of the new bogie saloons and four wheeled passenger brake leaving Knott End past the new signal box and track work. *R. Kidner*

Knott End Station looking towards the buffer stops showing the locomotive release crossover. *LGRP. Courtesy David & Charles*

supplies. At the foot of the hump, the goods line divided into two long sidings, the first of which passed immediately behind the station platform, and from this siding a crossover connected with the main line. The second siding, widely separated from the first, passed the cattle dock and a long brick building which served as a goods warehouse, running to a dead end opposite a large private warehouse. The main line had a loop through the station, which had two platforms, singling again to a dead end against the hedge bordering the main Lancaster–Blackpool road. This was the position up to 1908, and again since 1950. On the opening of the Knott End extension in 1908, the dead end was taken out and the line continued over the road by a level crossing, and a further short siding was laid in beyond the crossing to serve the warehouse of the Preston Farmers' Association. The crossing was in an extremely awkward situation, as there was a junction with a secondary road and a completely blind corner immediately beyond it, though owing to the lie of the land, and the position of cottages, there was no alternative.

The passenger station consisted of a long low brick building with a slate roof, and possessing no particular outstanding points. This was on the down platform, nearer to the western end, and the booking office was at the end of the building nearest the level crossing. Beyond were a small store, and the stationmaster's house. On the up platform was a simple open-fronted waiting shed, of wood, with a longitudinal bench inside. This platform was rarely used, except when required for crossing two trains, and has now fallen into ruin, the down platform being generally used for trains in both directions. Just beyond the level crossing was milepost 7, giving the distance from Garstang and Catterall. Since the withdrawal of passenger services, the down platform has suffered considerably from senile decay, and is now in a very crumbling state, though the buildings have fared rather better.

On the extension to Knott End, the only intermediate station was Preesall. At this place was a wonder of wonders—the only hill in the whole district. Indeed it was little more than a large mound, and there may be some truth in the local belief that it was an old British " barrow " or burial ground, but nobody is likely to establish the truth of this belief, since the village is built upon it. Nearby, in a field by the Blackpool road, formerly stood one of the two windmills in the district (the other one was at Pilling), the tallest in the Fylde area, with sails 38 feet long. It was built of brick in 1839, to replace a former wooden " post " mill which was blown down in the great gale of January 1839. It has

Knott End Station in 1930 with goods train headed by LMS No. 8525 0-6-0 shunting in the station area.
LGRP. Courtesy David & Charles

Knott End Station looking towards Preesall, the station master's house (left centre), the water tower and signal box in the distance.
LGRP. Courtesy David & Charles

been dismantled for some years, but the remnant of Pilling mill still stands in the village near the station, though hardly recognisable for what it was, for in 1870 it was converted to steam power, and the top section taken off.

Preesall station was a small affair, more occupied with goods than passengers. To the north of the station was a very large pond, fed by a brook, all this being within the boundaries of railway property. Though the station had only one platform, on the down side, there was a long loop opposite, and a pair of sidings passing behind the platform. One of these, serving the goods shed, was immediately behind the platform, and terminated in a dead end against the end of the station building. The other passed behind the goods shed, and was separated from it by a gravel roadway.

The station building was entirely of wood, with vertical boarding, having an awning over the platform, and a smaller awning over the entrance door at the other side. Apart from Knott End, this was the only station with a direct entrance from the roadway, in all other cases it was necessary to go on to the platform before entering the booking office. Nothing now remains of Preesall station except the platform, all buildings having been demolished. The road bridge still remains, though filled in, as its removal would be a work of some magnitude, not to say expense. The track bed from Pilling through to Knott End is easily traced even today. Portions have been ploughed back into the land from which it came; other sections have been covered by henhouses, this being great country for poultry farming. The diminutive crossing-keepers' houses of the Knott End extension survive as private dwelling places, and much of the route west of Preesall is still fenced off (with the old posts !) and used as a local footpath.

Leaving Preesall, the line continued its straight and level course for a short distance, then curving gently north-westwards, passed the golf links, and receiving the short salt-works branch on the left (the junction facing towards Knott End), entered the terminus, $4\frac{1}{2}$ miles from Pilling. Knott End was the most extensive yard on the line, the railway boundaries enclosing a considerable area, and it had also the most substantial buildings. Approaching from Preesall on a slight curve, the line doubled, and immediately threw off to the left a branch to the goods yard, which though very extensive in area, had only two sidings. The goods shed was a substantial brick building with a wide platform and a crane, the siding being on the side facing the river. The goods shed still stands, isolated in the old yard. Beyond a strip of track ballast disappears into the boskage to mark the former route to Pilling, and around the terminus itself a recent spate of housing has altered the old environment. The second siding ran along the back of the platform of the passenger station. The double main line continued into the passenger station up to the buffer stops, two crossovers being provided for run-round purposes. Just off the end of the platform stood the only signal the station possessed, which served as a starter for not only the passenger lines but the goods yard as well. A water tower and coal bin were placed by the signal post. Incidentally, the water tower was moved at some period to the outer end of the down platform, where it remained until the line was dismantled. Beyond the coal bin were two sidings leading to the two-road carriage shed, constructed in the usual wood and corrugated iron. This was demolished soon after passenger traffic ceased. A small signal box stood opposite, and adjacent to the carriage shed was the stationmaster's house, which still remains, though not now in possession of a railway servant.

The station itself stood close to the promenade at Knott End, and near the ferry landing whence a regular daily ferry service was provided across the river to Fleetwood, operated by Fleetwood Corporation. From the goods yard there was an extensive view of the quays and docks of Fleetwood, and the L. & Y.R. station, which was alongside the quay. Knott End station building was a pleasant structure of bright red brick, the upper portions of the walls being pebble-dashed. The building was arranged across the platform ends, and consisted of a central portion with a wing at each end placed at right angles, the two wings being of unequal length. The booking office was in the centre, with straight through access to the circulating area. As first built, the circulating area was entirely open, but at some period later, a huge glass screen, with glass roof and brickwork ends, was erected to cover it. This was pulled down soon after passenger services were withdrawn. The two platforms were entirely open, and there was no shelter of any kind on them, nor were there any lamps.

For some years now, the building has been in use as a cafe, with sundry minor alterations to the exterior, but until the complete closure of the line in 1950, the railway retained the eastern wing as a parcels office. (The sign-board still remained on the wall until 1959 at least.) This has now become a waiting room for the Ribble bus services operating from Knott End. The goods shed still stands, as does the stationmaster's house ; the goods yard is now a car park, and the course of the line, though still traceable, is rapidly disappearing in the surrounding boskage.

8. LOCOMOTIVES

Line drawings of all the locomotives used on the line are provided but it must be emphasised that those of " Hebe ", " Union " and " Hope " may not be correct in all details, since no illustrations of these engines have survived, and few details, so that drawings have had to be made from details of similar locomotives. As far as possible the builders' records have been consulted, and engines as near as ascertainable identical have been used in making the drawings. With the remaining stock, the drawings can be taken as accurate, having been made from diagrams provided through the courtesy of the builders, and dimensional details from the records of British Railways.

HEBE

This, the first engine on the line, was built by Black, Hawthorn & Co. of Gateshead-on-Tyne in 1870, works number 118. It was an 0-4-2 saddle tank, one of the builders' stock designs, and apart from the coupled wheel diameter and wheelbase, was very similar to an engine delivered to the Isle of Wight Central Railway in the same year, works number 116. It went from Knott End in 1872 to J. P. Radley, then Lea Green Colliery, and about 1898 to T. Mitchell of Bolton, a dealer. The coupled wheels were 3′ 6″ diameter, with a pair of trailing wheels 2′ 6″, the wheelbase being 5′ 6″ + 5′ 0″. The outside cylinders were 13″ × 18″, driving the rear coupled axle ; the coupling and connecting rods had plain bushed ends. In boiler power, the engine was decidedly on the small side, having a total heating surface of only 321 sq. ft., and working pressure 120 lb. The saddle tank covered the boiler only, and held 400 gallons ; the small rear bunker provided space for 15 cwt. of coal. A cab, of sorts, was provided, but was little more than a roof plate supported by front and back weatherboards, typical of the makers' practice for small industrial locomotives at this period. In common with most small engines designed for industrial use, the boiler was domeless, the dome being placed on the raised firebox, and surmounted by a pair of Salter valves. Hand brakes only were fitted, operating wooden blocks at the rear of the coupled wheels. Buffer height was only three feet above the rails, and on this account for many years the rolling stock was all fitted with buffing gear at this height, instead of the standard railway height of 3′ 6″. For this reason,

The Garstang & Knott End Railway

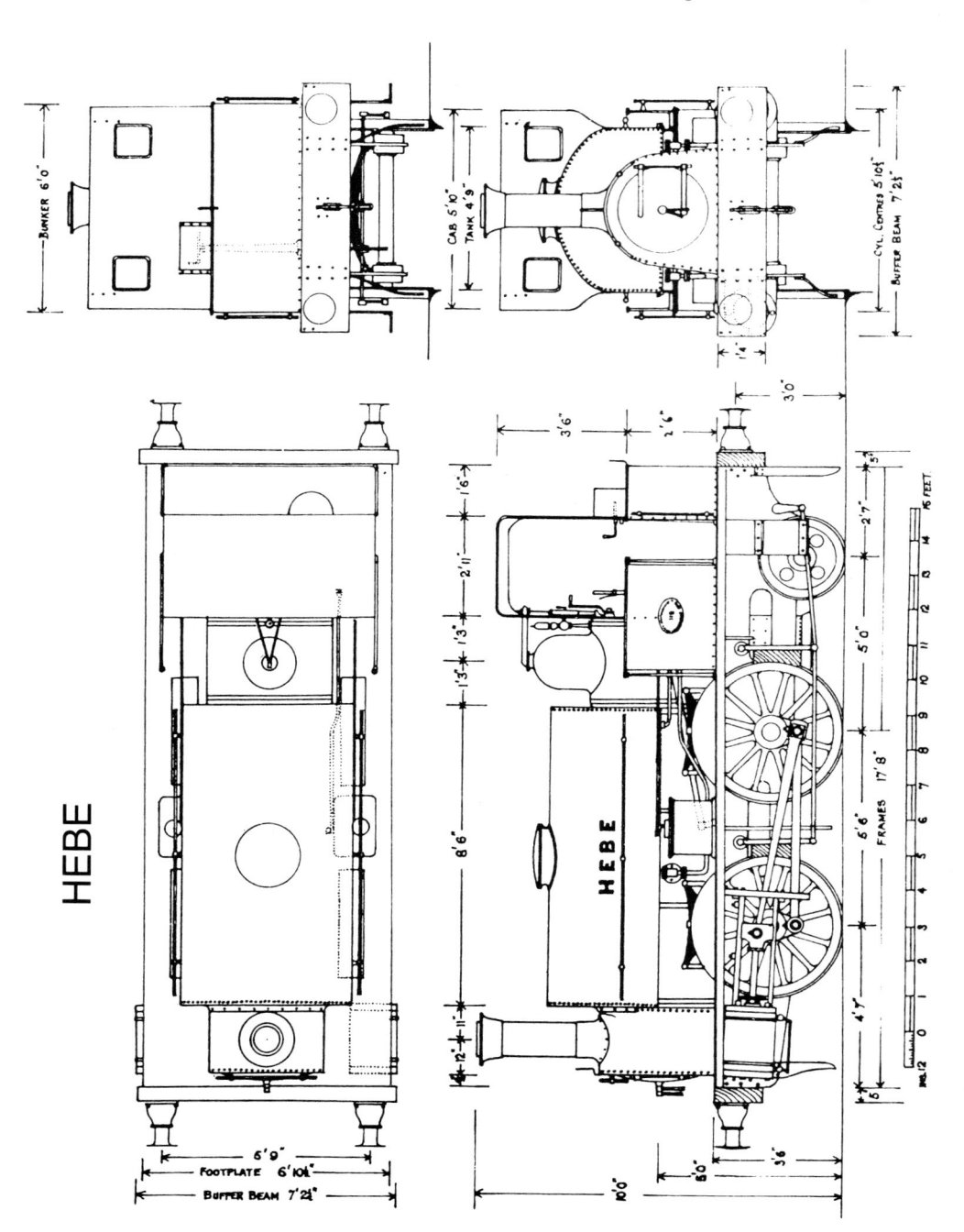

HEBE

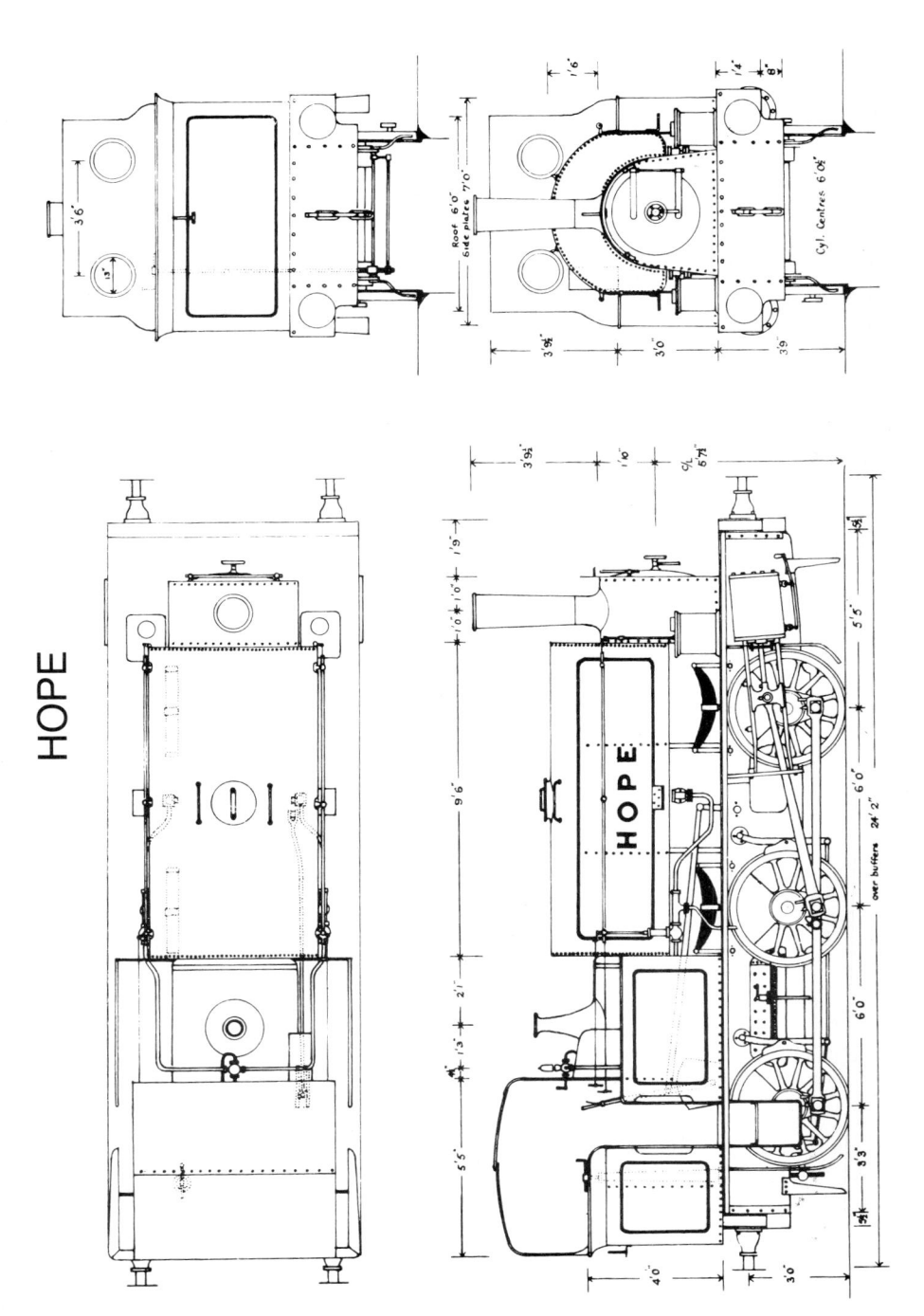

HOPE

Blackpool 2–6–0T with crew and inspector in 1939. R. Kidner

Jubilee Queen and brake van No. 1 photographed here at Knott End. R. Kidner

a good deal of transhipment of loads was necessary at Garstang and Catterall, as Knott End wagons could not be coupled into L.N.W.R. trains. This defect was remedied in the late 1890's by the introduction of standard buffing gear, and the fitting of larger diameter wheels to some of the goods stock.

Despite her small dimensions, " Hebe " performed wonders on the line, as we have seen earlier, and it is only natural that after two years of such intensive work the boiler was in such a parlous state when the line was closed in 1872.

UNION

The second engine, obtained in 1875 for the re-opening of the traffic, was a standard contractor's type 0-4-0 saddle tank of Manning Wardle's build, purchased secondhand from James Pilling, the contractor who built the Lancashire Union Railway (from Chorley to Cherry Tree Junction, Blackburn) a joint undertaking of the Lancashire & Yorkshire and London & North Western Railways. The engine had been built in 1868, and was number 226 in the makers' list. It was a design of which the makers constructed several hundred examples in various sizes, a design which was virtually unchanged except in details, throughout the existence of the firm. Its outside cylinders were $9\frac{1}{2}'' \times 14''$, driving wheels of 2' 9" diameter on a wheelbase of 5' 0". The domeless boiler had a diameter of 2' 11" outside, and was 7' 0" long, working at 120 lb. pressure, and contained 78 tubes of 2" diameter. Total heating surface was 319 sq. ft., and grate area $9\frac{1}{2}$ sq. ft. The box-like saddle tank held 350 gallons of water, and space for 15 cwt. of coal was found in side bunkers. The firebox was of the usual raised type with a large dome, surmounted by a pair of Salter safety valves. No cab was fitted, merely a front weatherboard. Buffer height of this engine was again 3' 0", but shortly before being sold, the buffer beams were altered to give a height of 3' 5". It is rather surprising that this engine was retained so long (probably owing to lack of funds) as it was by no means suited to the work required of it, being underpowered, and, by the small diameter of its wheels, very slow. In 1883, " Union " was disposed of to Hudswell Clarke & Co., in part exchange for the new engine " Hope". In all probability, Hudswell Clarke & Co. never actually brought the engine into their works, having resold it almost immediately, for shortly afterwards " Union " was working for the Fleetwood Salt Co., within a short distance of its former surroundings. Here it remained until 1898, when it was disposed of to Wilson Lovatt & Sons Ltd., a firm of contractors, and its subsequent history is lost.

Knott End 0–6–0 Manning Wardle, No. 1732 built in 1908, photographed here in September 1939. *R. Kidner*

Blackpool 2–6–0T and *New Century* 0–6–0ST seen here at Garstang Town. *R. Kidner*

The Garstang & Knott End Railway 61

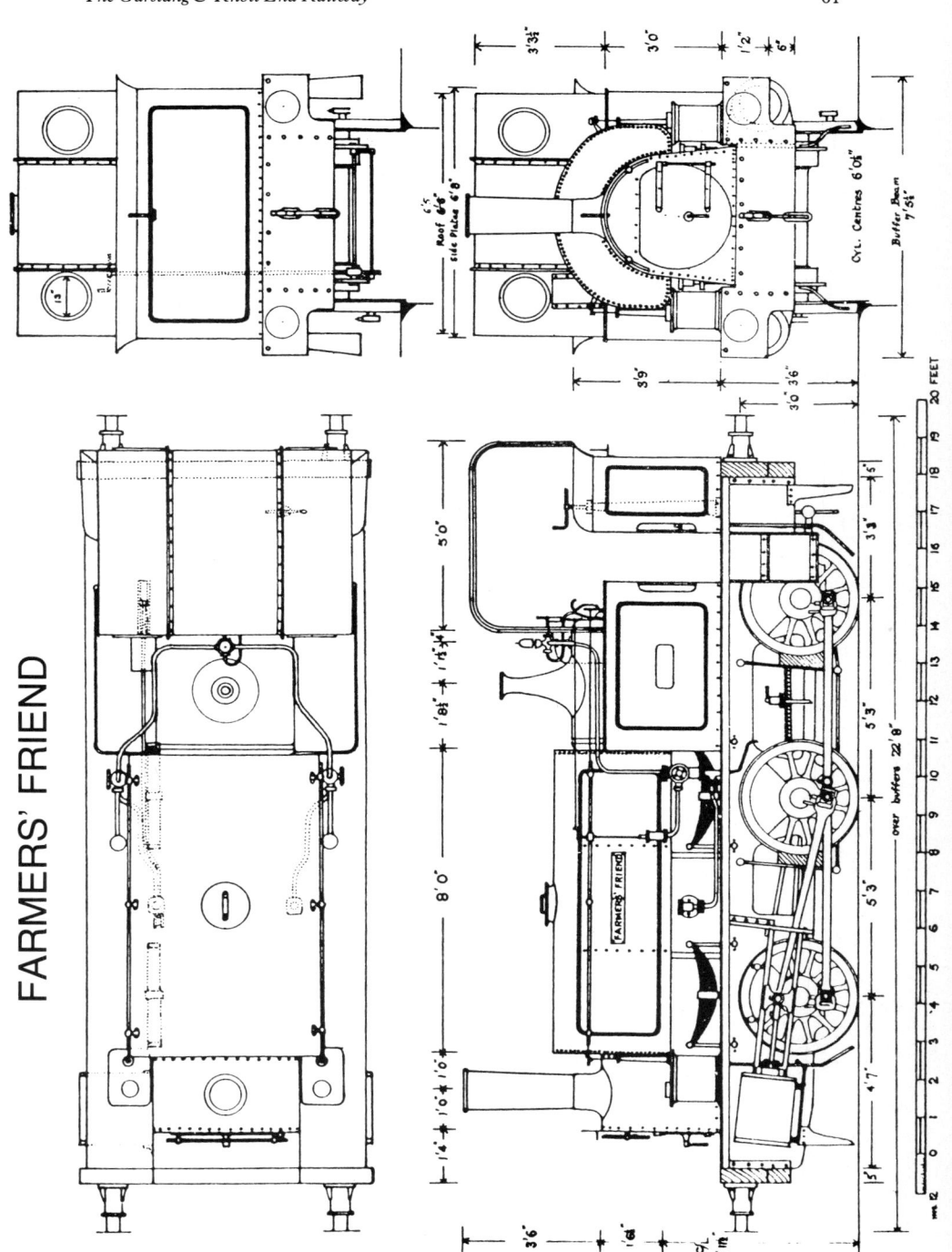

FARMERS' FRIEND

62   *The Garstang & Knott End Railway*

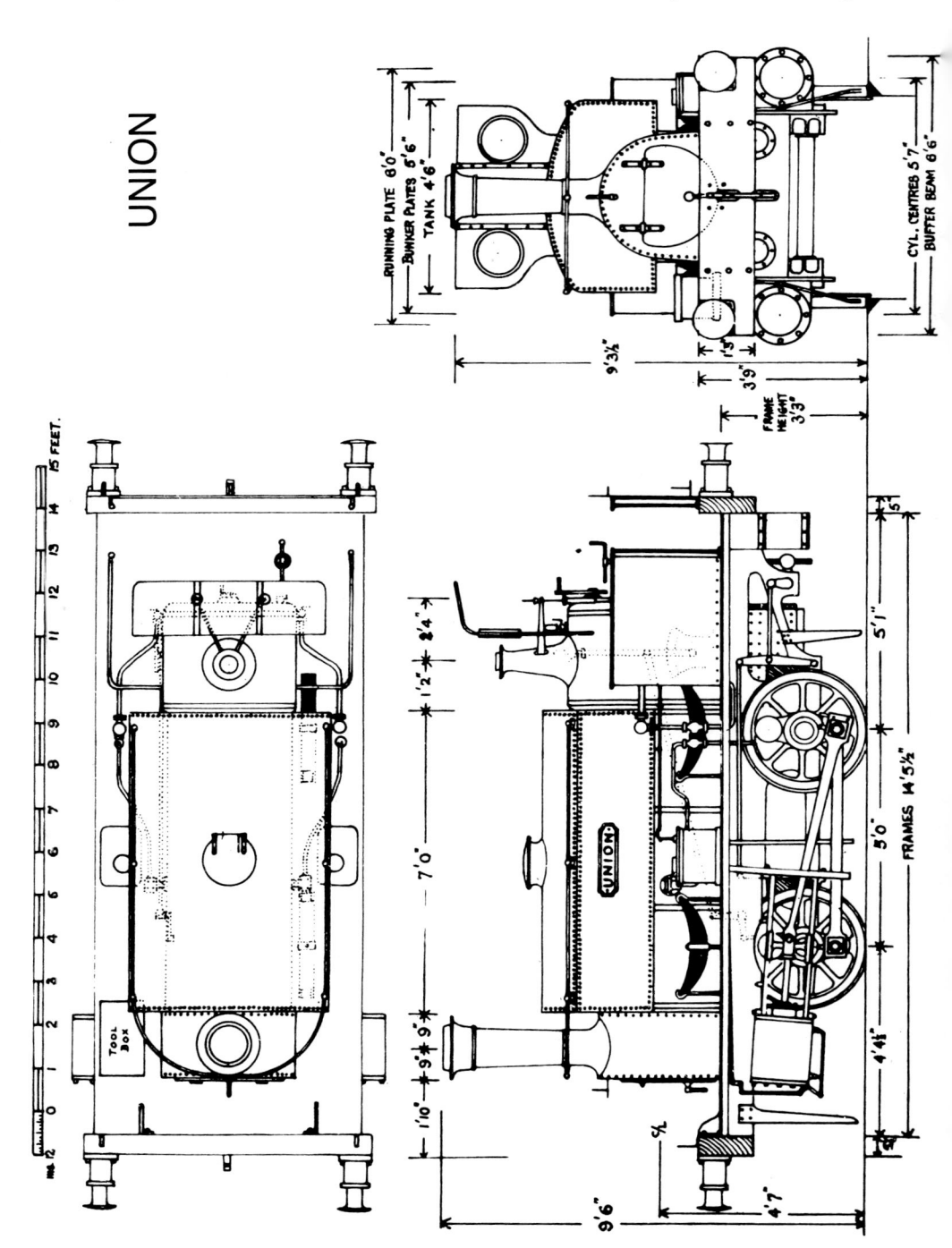

The Garstang & Knott End Railway

FARMERS' FRIEND

There is some doubt as to the correct position of the apostrophe in the name of this engine; some authorities place it before the " s ". In the absence of any confirmative photograph, it seems irrelevant whether the farmer were singular or plural; anyway, as the old Cockney saying goes, " you pays yer money and takes yer choice ". Incidentally, a Locomotive Publishing Co. photograph which has been in circulation for many years, purporting to be " Farmers' Friend ", is definitely not this engine, but a similar one, built for a colliery in the Midlands. Comparison of this photograph with the builders' official dimensions proves that they do not agree in several particulars. Perkins used this photograph to illustrate " Farmers' Friend " in his article in the *Railway Magazine* in 1908 (probably in all good faith)—and it is there that the confusion has almost certainly arisen.

The engine was delivered in December 1875, and was Hudswell, Clarke's number 173. It was an 0-6-0 saddle tank, by far the most suitable design the railway had had up to that time. The outside cylinders were 11" × 17", wheels 3' 0", on a wheelbase of 10' 6", equally divided. Not all the dimensions are available, but the boiler was 3' 0" diameter and 8' 4" in length, working at 120 lb. The number of tubes and heating surface are not known. The saddle tank held 500 gallons. Again the boiler was domeless, but in this case there was no dome on the raised firebox, only a pair of safety valves in a tall polished brass cover of the makers' usual pattern. A sheet-iron roof, strengthened with angle iron, covered the footplate and enclosed the bunker, but there was no side protection from the weather. Coupling and connecting rods were fitted with cottered brasses. Full front and back sanding was provided, with sandboxes above the footplate—a noticeable improvement on the earlier engines, whose sanding arrangements were of the hit-and-miss variety, being merely a straight pipe delivering sand midway between the coupled wheels. " Farmers' Friend " gave yeoman service in the twenty odd years it was on the line, and its advent relegated the little four-wheeled " Union " to the status of spare engine. In 1897, " Farmers' Friend " went back to its birthplace in part exchange for a new engine, and was sold to J. F. Howard of Bedford about 1900.

HOPE

This engine was very similar to the previous one, but differed in details, being on the whole slightly larger. It was also a Hudswell, Clarke product, being their number 263 of 1883. The cylinders, 13" ×

Jubilee Queen at Garstang Town shed. Built by Hudswell Clarke and Co, Leeds in 1897, and works No. 484. LMS number allocation was 11300.   *R. Kidner*

Knott End 0-6-0, Manning Wardle No. 1732 built 1908 seen here on the 28th September 1923.   *R. Kidner*

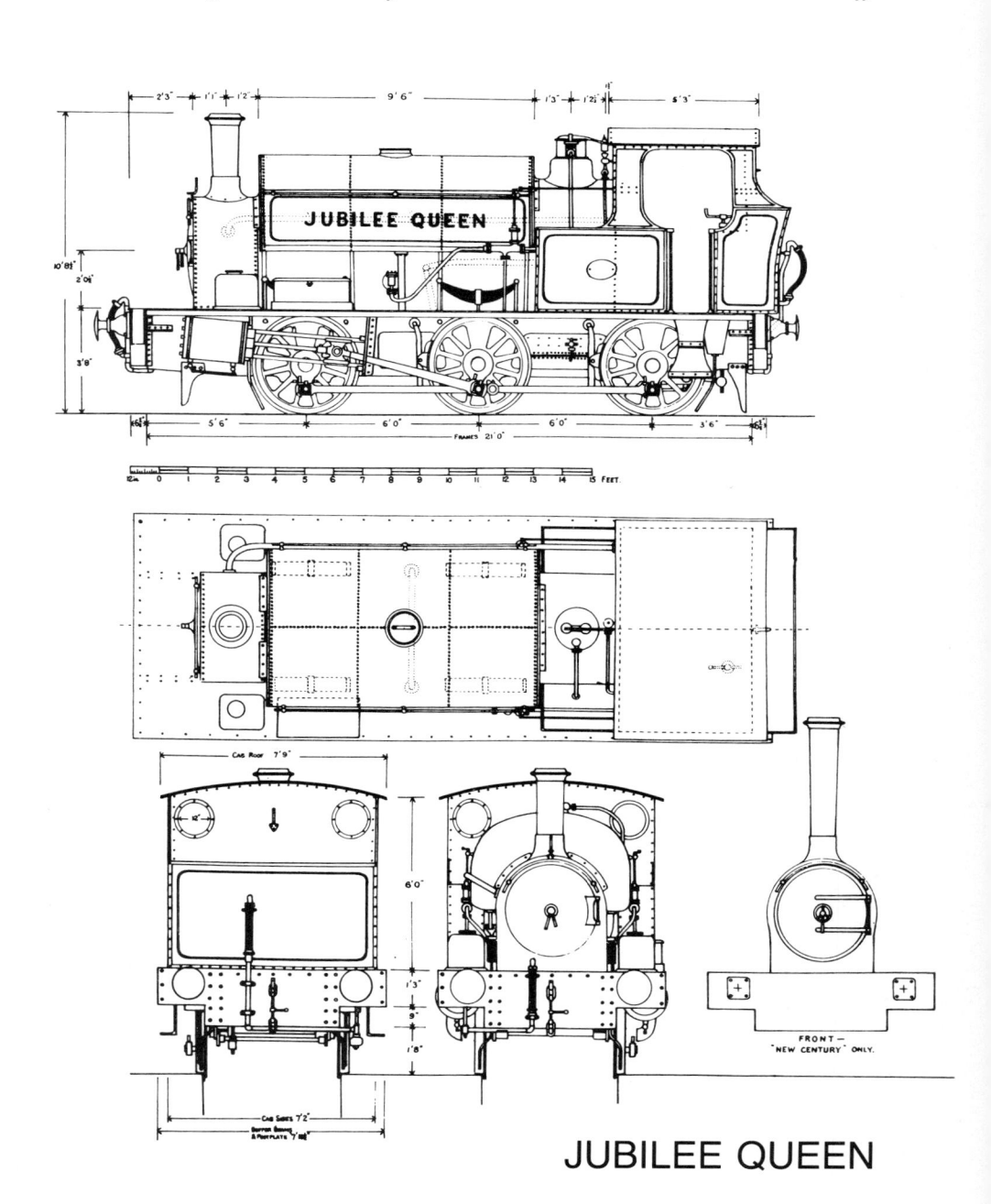

JUBILEE QUEEN

20", were outside the frames, and actuated by Stephenson link motion. Coupled wheels were 3' 6" diameter, on a wheelbase of 12' 0", equally divided. General layout was as in " Farmers' Friend," the bunker, however, being rather larger, and projecting 6" beyond the rear buffer beam. The cab roof was formed of two plates, overlapped and rivetted in the centre, and was narrower than the side sheets, the weatherboards being curved outwards and downwards at their lower ends to meet them. This was the first engine since " Hebe " to have a dished smokebox door. The boiler was 3' 0" diameter and 9' 6" long, working at 120 lb., and having 81 tubes of 2" diameter, which gave 403 sq. ft. of heating surface. The firebox added a further 61 sq. ft., giving a total of 464 sq. ft. Water capacity of the saddle tank was 500 gallons, and the bunker held $1\frac{1}{2}$ tons of coal. Buffer height was again 3' 0". There was a hand brake only, actuating iron blocks on the driving and trailing wheels. " Hope " was taken back by the makers in 1900 in part exchange for " New Century " and sold to T. Mitchell of Bolton, a dealer.

JUBILEE QUEEN and NEW CENTURY

These two engines were identical, except in minor details and were Hudswell, Clarke's numbers 484 of 1897, and 559 of 1900. In size, they were again larger than " Hope ", but of the same general outline. Their outside cylinders were 15" × 20", wheels 3' 6", and wheelbase 12' 0", equally divided. Buffer beams were of the sandwich type, a $5\frac{1}{4}$" baulk of wood faced each side by a $\frac{5}{16}$" steel plate. " Jubilee Queen " had her buffers mounted directly on the beams, but " New Century " had a 3" block of wood, square in section, interposed. All the minor differences between the two engines were at the front end, and are perhaps better tabulated :

There seems to be no particular reason for the extra long chimney on " New Century " ; it certainly gave the engine a rather ungainly look. It must have been a later addition, but there is no proof when, as most available photographs of the engine show the long chimney. The mechanical lubricators are likewise thought to be a later addition.

Both engines were domeless, with raised fireboxes. The boiler was the largest yet employed, 3' 5" diameter and 9' 3" long, fitted with $119 \times 1\frac{1}{2}$" tubes, and working at 140 lb. pressure. Heating surface was 593·45 sq. ft. in the tubes, 67·04 sq. ft. in the firebox, giving a total of 660·49 sq. ft. Grate area was 10·62 sq. ft. The bunker, which projected over the rear buffer beam, held $1\frac{1}{2}$ tons of coal, and the saddle tank provided 750 gallons of water. A full cab was fitted, with side

The Garstang & Knott End Railway

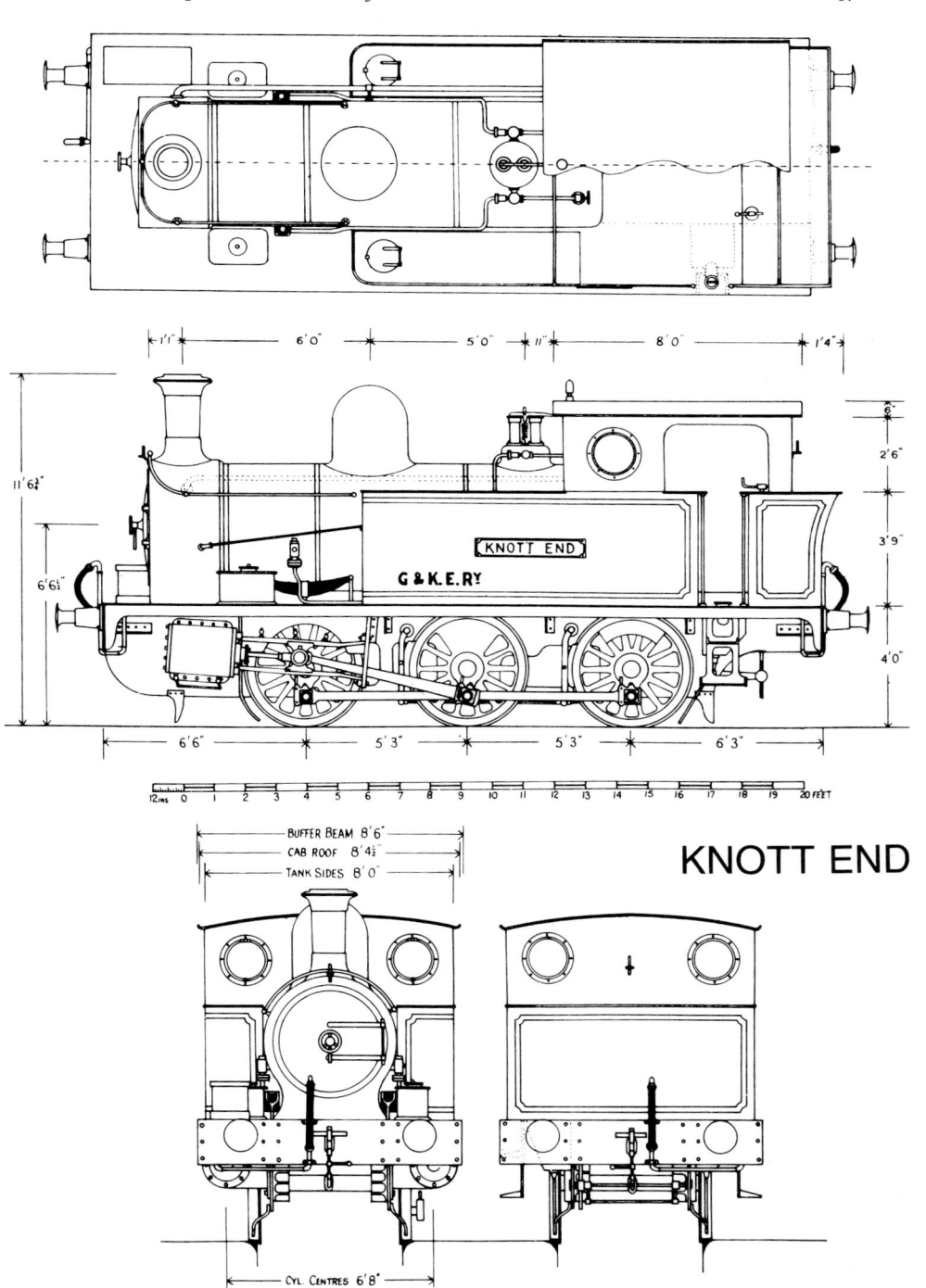

KNOTT END

2–6–0 side tank *Blackpool* with crew and inspector etc. F. Moore Postcard

0–6–0 saddle tank *New Century* at the coaling stage. F. Moore Postcard

sheets, the best protection from the weather so far. The rear spectacle plate was set in 6" from the rear of the side sheets; its position is shown in the drawing by a line of rivets. When built, the engines were fitted with hand and steam brakes; the continuous automatic vacuum brake was added in 1908, after the arrival of the new passenger stock. Though most, if not all, the rolling stock at this time had a buffer height of 3' 0", the engines had their buffers at 3' 3" above rails. Only one lamp bracket was fitted at each end.

When the L.M.S.R. took over in 1923, "Jubilee Queen" and "New Century" were allotted numbers 11300 and 11301 respectively. "New Century" never received the number, but its sister was overhauled and repainted at Crewe in 1924, and was numbered 11300 at the same time. Both engines were scrapped at Crewe, 11300 in March 1926, and 11301 in October 1925.

	"Jubilee Queen"	"New Century"
Smokebox	D-shaped.	Slightly narrower at bottom.
Smokebox door	2 handles, plate hinges.	Handle and wheel, strap hinges.
Chimney height	10" 8½'	12' 6"
Toolbox	On nearside running plate.	In cab.
Other details	——	Mechanical lubricator on both sides, worked from crossheads.

Knott End

For the opening of the extension to Knott End in 1908, a new engine was purchased. This time it was a complete breakaway from previous practice, both as to type and manufacture. "Knott End" was an 0-6-0 side tank, designed and built by Manning, Wardle & Co., of Leeds, being number 1732 of 1908 in their books. Though it was one of the makers' stock designs, the side tank variety was not very common, the bulk of their production being saddle tanks. It showed all the typical Manning Wardle features, most noticeable being the smokebox, side tanks with rounded front corners, and the handrail curving up above the smokebox. The cylinder and wheel dimensions—14" × 20" and 3' 9"—were also one of the builders' standards. The cylinders were outside, and the wheelbase was 10' 6", equally divided. The boiler was 3' 11" diameter and 8' 0" long, working at 150 lb. and containing $157 \times 1\frac{3}{4}$" tubes. Heating surface was 556·4 sq. ft. + 62·6, total 610 sq. ft., with a grate area of 10 sq. ft. The side tanks held 700 gallons, and the bunker 1½ tons of coal.

BLACKPOOL

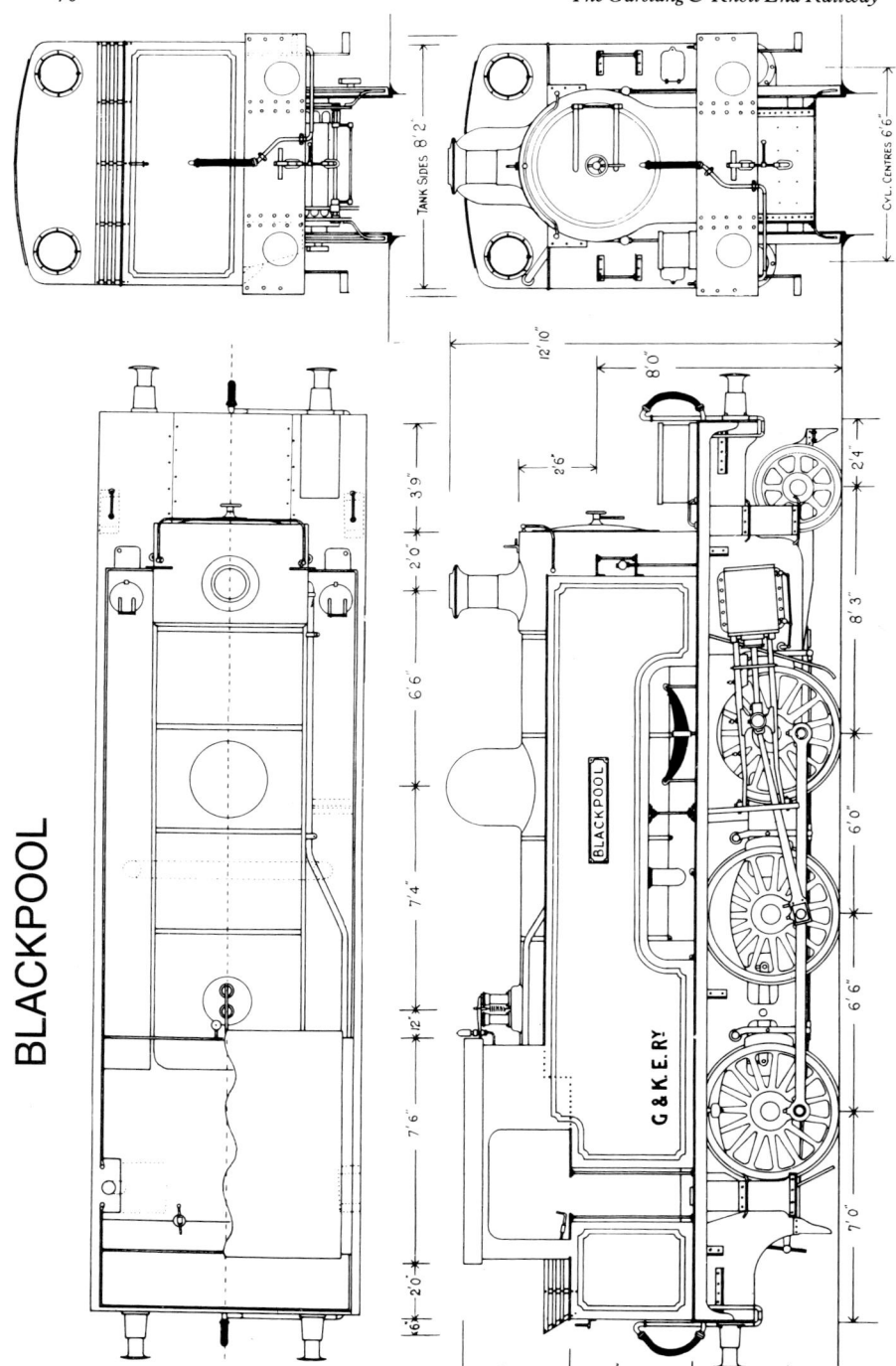

Tank tops were sunk 6″ below the top beading, the fillers thus not being visible from the side, and an unusual feature was the circular " porthole " in the cab side. Vacuum brakes were fitted when built, the ejector pipe passing along the right side of the boiler, while the train pipe was hidden behind the footplate valance, also on the right side. A large toolbox occupied the front right-hand corner of the running plate, and in accordance with G. & K.E.R. practice, there was only one lamp iron at each end. Only in the cab footsteps was there any departure from the builders' standard practice—for some reason these were of G.W.R. open pattern, Manning, Wardle's usual pattern being solid.

In 1923, " Knott End" was allotted L.M.S. number 11302, which it never carried, being broken up at Horwich in June 1924.

BLACKPOOL

Shortly after the acquisition of " Knott End", a further locomotive was placed in service, named " Blackpool ", and also purchased from Manning, Wardle & Co. (1747 of 1909). This time, however, it was not a standard design of the makers, and indeed was of a type which almost succeeded in being unique, on standard gauge lines in this country at least, though there was one standard gauge 2-6-0 tank in Ireland. It is not clear who was responsible for the design of this engine ; several features shout aloud " Manning, Wardle ", notably the smokebox, cylinders, and the design of cab and rear portion of the side tanks. Probably the railway company outlined the type and capabilities of the engine, and the builders worked out the details. It was the largest locomotive the company ever had, and was intended for goods traffic, though it frequently worked passenger trains as well.

" Blackpool " was a massive-looking engine, with very long side tanks which reached almost to the front of the smokebox, and were cut away in the centre to allow access to the motion. Just above the motion plate on each side was a built-up bracket (consisting of a flat plate with four angle irons bolted to it) which gave extra support to the tanks in the cut-away part. The tank tops were sunk 6″ below the top beading, and in view of their height, a footstep incorporating a handrail was fitted at the front ends. The front sandboxes were in the bottom of the side tanks, access to them being by a small flap in the tank end plates. The tanks were not shaped to fit the boiler, although looking from the front, they would appear so ; the space at the front was filled in by a gusset plate. The running plate was raised to clear the coupled wheels, necessitating a very deep buffer beam. As with " Knott End ", the vacuum brake train pipe was carried along the back of the running plate valance on the right-hand side, and the ejector pipe along the right-hand tank top. Isaacson's patent valve gear was fitted.

The cab was unusual for a Manning, Wardle engine. Although it had the typical general lines, the roof was curved down into the side-sheets without overhanging eaves, rather in the fashion of Midland Railway design. The chimney was placed close to the smokebox tube-plate, giving the effect of an extended smokebox. Driving and trailing coupled wheel springs were compensated. The leading axle was a Bissell truck, built up in box form from plate and angle, the front guard irons being merely a shaped steel strip bent over at the ends, and bolted to a short angle-iron extension of the side frames. The springs were inside, above the axleboxes.

Coupled wheels were 4' 0" diameter, and leading wheels 2' 9½". The outside cylinders were 16" × 22", and the wheelbase 20' 9", divided 8' 3" + 6' 0" + 6' 6". The boiler was 4' 5" diameter and 10' 0" long, working at 150 lb. There were 180 tubes of 1¾" diameter, which gave 832·4 sq. ft. heating surface. The firebox added a further 69·6 sq. ft., making the total 902 sq. ft. Grate area was 14½ sq. ft. The tanks carried 1000 gallons of water, and the bunker 2 tons of coal.

" Blackpool " was allotted L.M.S.R. number 11680 in 1923, being classified as a goods engine. In 1924 it was overhauled and repainted at Crewe, and remained in service until October 1927, thus being the last G. & K.E.R. locomotive. It suffered from a certain amount of un-steadiness, particularly when running bunker first. This was said to be due partly to the high build of the locomotive, and partly to the leading truck, which being of the Bissell type without side-control, did not steady the locomotive as it should. It was proposed to alter the truck to a spring-controlled pony when the engine was overhauled at Crewe in 1924, but being a solitary example, the expense was not thought worthwhile.

The early demise of the locomotives necessitated bringing in fresh types, and after several trials, L. & Y. 0-6-2 tanks were found to be the most suitable all-round locomotives for the line, aided by L.N.W.R. " Cauliflower " 0-6-0 tender engines. The passenger services were maintained chiefly by the L.N.W.R. rail motor, previously mentioned, though the 0-6-2 tanks were used as well. The L. & Y. engines, built in the early 1880's, were themselves due for withdrawal and on their demise, the " Cauliflowers " held almost undisputed sway until after

New Century at Garstang Town shed. Built by Hudswell Clarke and Co, Leeds in 1900, and works No. 559. LMS number allocation was 11301.   *R. Kidner*

On shed at Garstang Town with locomotive *New Century* simmering after a day's work.
  R. Kidner

the last war. Since then, any available engine has been employed on the daily pick-up goods, from L. & Y. 0-6-0's to Stanier Class 5's. Latterly, an unusual vehicle has appeared; a hand-crane, of L. & Y. origin, mounted on a flat wagon. This spends most of its time in Pilling yard, since Pilling goods shed was never equipped with a crane.

FLEETWOOD SALT Co.

This company, which built the new works at Preesall, and also the older chemical works at Burn Naze, Fleetwood, became part of the United Alkali Company about the time that the Preesall plant came into operation, and finally was absorbed into the great I.C.I. combine. The Burn Naze works had its own internal railway and when the Preesall works were built, at least two locomotives were transferred there, to work the mineral branch which joined the G. & K.E.R. near Knott End. The main works was closed about 1925, when the pipeline was installed under the river to Burn Naze, but Preesall Mine remained in use some years, finally closing about 1933 or 1934. Four locomotives appear to have worked at Preesall, though whether all four were there at the same time is a moot point. Apart from shunting in the works yard, their duties included working two special trains daily into Knott End yard.

The four engines engaged at Preesall were "Union", ex-G. & K.E.R., which has already been dealt with; "Ajax", "Sir Max", and "Henderson". Of these, the first two were transferred from other works of the company, while "Henderson" was purchased from a contractor, J. Waddell. "Ajax" was an inside-cylindered 0-6-0 saddle tank, built by Manning, Wardle & Co. in 1864, works number 128. It came to Preesall from the Hutchinson Works of the United Alkali Co. at Widnes, and was finally scrapped about 1925. "Sir Max" was also a Manning, Wardle product, No. 502 of 1874, but was an outside-cylindered 0-4-0 saddle tank, very similar in general appearance to "Union". It came from the works of Muspratt Bros. & Huntley, of Flint, North Wales, which was also part of the United Alkali Co. In 1933, just before the final closure, it was transferred to the Gaskell Marsh Works, Widnes. "Henderson", the last engine to come to Preesall, was also the last to leave. It was an outside-cylindered 0-4-0 saddle tank built by Andrew Barclay & Sons, of Kilmarnock, works No. 290 of 1892. Purchased from J. Waddell, at some date unknown, it finally went in 1934 to A. Kenneth & Sons, of Dreghorn, near Kilmarnock. With the departure of "Henderson", the Knott End Railway finally severed all connection with the Preesall Works.

All four of these engines were standard industrial types of their respective makers, and several identical duplicates of them can still be seen in active service in various parts of the country. Unfortunately, no details of the livery of any of them have been handed down.

9. PASSENGER ROLLING STOCK

The original passenger coaches of 1870, four in number, were of a distinctly unusual design, though who drew up the specifications is not at all clear. It is thought that Hamand had a finger in the pie somewhere—which might explain the unusual design—though probably the main plans were drawn up by the builders, the Metropolitan Carriage & Wagon Co. Running on six wheels, they were low-slung, and were one of the earliest examples of saloon coaches with centre gangways. There were no side doors, access being by open end-platforms (extremely narrow, be it noted). The wheels were of spoked wagon pattern, 2' 10" diameter, on a wheelbase of 20' 0", the centre axle being allowed a fair amount of sideplay. Probably the low height of the underframes was made to suit the buffer height of the earlier locomotives. However, in 1897, when the first of the permanent locomotives was obtained, the coaches were " modernised " (if that is the right word !) to a certain extent, the buffer beams being raised, Mansell wheels of 3' 6" diameter fitted, and the first class seats upholstered, instead of being merely covered with blue repp, as they were originally. The third class seating remained plain wood. All four coaches lasted until 1909, when they were broken up.

Actually there were two varieties, a third class only, and a first-third composite, two coaches of each type. The composite is illustrated fully in the drawings, the all-third is shown only in the main points of difference. In all essentials, the two types were alike, the difference being that the all-thirds were two feet shorter, though the wheelbase was the same. All were straight sided, with four drop windows each side ; over each drop window was a louvre ventilator. Strictly speaking, they were not louvres as is understood by that term today, but rather a sort of wooden grille, as they were formed of a wooden frame filled with horizontal slats. The end doors opened inwards. There were no continuous brakes, the hand brake being applied by means of a wheel at the end of each coach. In the composites, the brake wheel was fitted in the first class saloon, which was separated from the third class accommodation by a bulkhead with central door. Lighting was

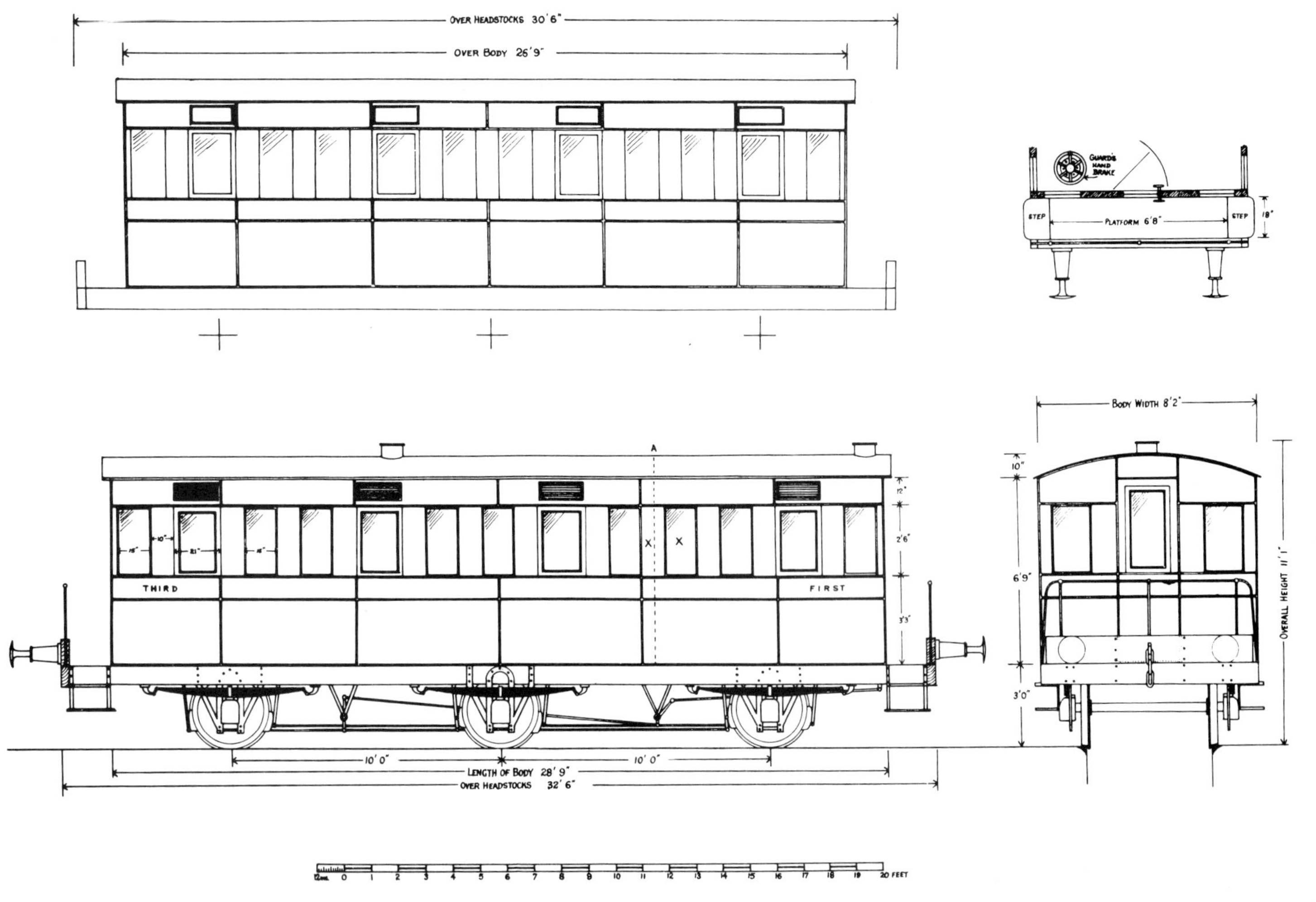

OVER HEADSTOCKS 30'6"
OVER BODY 26'9"
GUARD'S HAND BRAKE
STEP
PLATFORM 6'8"
STEP
18"
BODY WIDTH 8'2"
A
12"
2'6"
3'3"
15"
10"
21"
15"
X
X
THIRD
FIRST
10"
6'9"
3'0"
OVERALL HEIGHT 11'1"
10'0"
10'0"
LENGTH OF BODY 28'9"
OVER HEADSTOCKS 32'6"
12ins 0 1 2 3 4 5 6 7 8 9 10 11 12 13 14 15 16 17 18 19 20 FEET

extremely poor ; only two oil lamps were provided, one at the centre of the third class saloon, the other at the platform end of the first class, presumably mainly for the benefit of the guard. In the all-thirds, the two lamps were in the same position. This sepulchral lighting was never improved. The seating arrangements are conjectural, as no details have survived.

In addition, there were two four-wheeled coaches obtained secondhand from the Mersey Railway about 1906, after that company had electrified its line. It is doubtful whether these were ever used, as they required considerable renovation, and before this had been carried out—or indeed commenced—the new bogie stock had been delivered, and it seems likely that they were broken up without ever having been in service.

When at long last, the line was extended to Knott End, eight new coaches were built by the Birmingham Railway Carriage and Wagon Co., and delivered in time for the opening. These were a considerable advance on the 1870 relics, though the general principle was the same, open saloons with centre gangways and end platforms. In appearance, they were very similar to contemporary American practice. They were straight sided, with 13 drop windows each side, and a glass ventilator over each hinged at the bottom and opening inwards. There was considerably more protection on the platforms, which were roofed over and provided with a substantial end railing and iron gates on each side. Access to the saloon was by a sliding door in the end bulkheads, placed 9" off centre. The automatic vacuum brake was fitted, but there was no provision for heating. Lighting was a big improvement on the old coaches, but still nothing to brag about, consisting of five gas lamps along the centre of the roof. Again there were two types, third class only, and first-third composites. (Second class was never catered for on the G. & K.E.R.). The composites had a bulkhead with centre door fitted between the fourth and fifth windows from one end, but externally both types were identical. The underframes were fitted with a pair of 7' 6" bogies at 31' 0" centres, the bogies having plate frames and transverse bolster springs.

The first class compartment seated 12, on longitudinal seats upholstered in brown leather, and having armrests between each seat. Third class accommodation was plain wood lath-and-space seats, arranged two and two transversely on either side of the central gangway, all seats except those against the bulkheads being of the reversible type. In the composites there were 35 third class seats, but the all-thirds

One of the bogie saloons standing in Knott End Station.   R. Kidner

One of the bogie coach bodies lying at rest and derelict at Garstang in 1963.   M. Price

One bogie coach saloon with the four-wheel passenger brake.

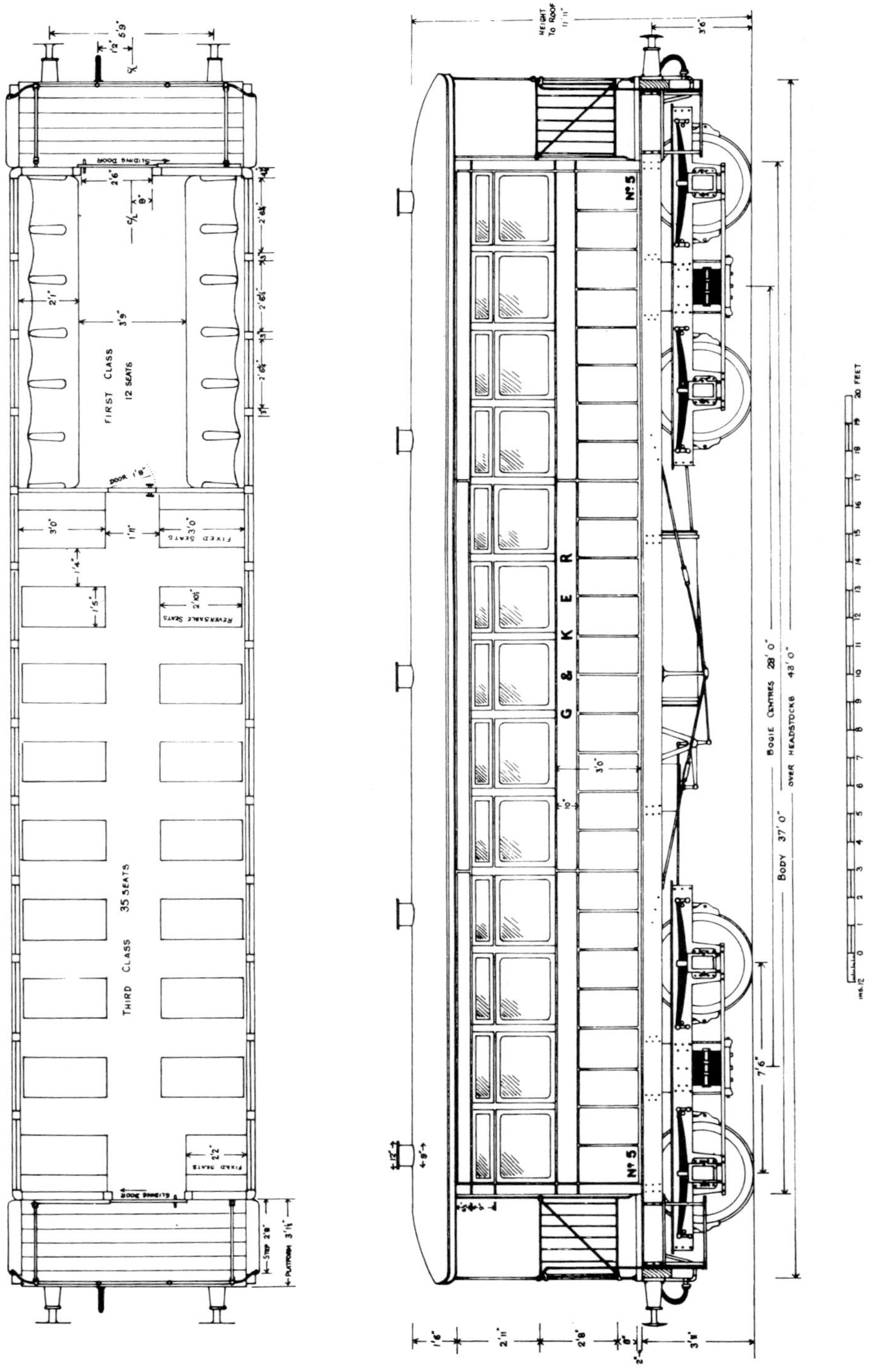

FIRST CLASS
12 SEATS
THIRD CLASS
35 SEATS
SLIDING DOOR
FIXED SEATS
REVERSABLE SEATS
G & K E R
Nº 5
HEIGHT TO ROOF 11' 11"
BOGIE CENTRES 28' 0"
OVER HEADSTOCKS 43' 0"
BODY 37' 0"
20 FEET

The Garstang & Knott End Railway bogie coach at Wanlockhead (1930) with the four wheeled brake passenger coach.
LGRP. Courtesy David & Charles

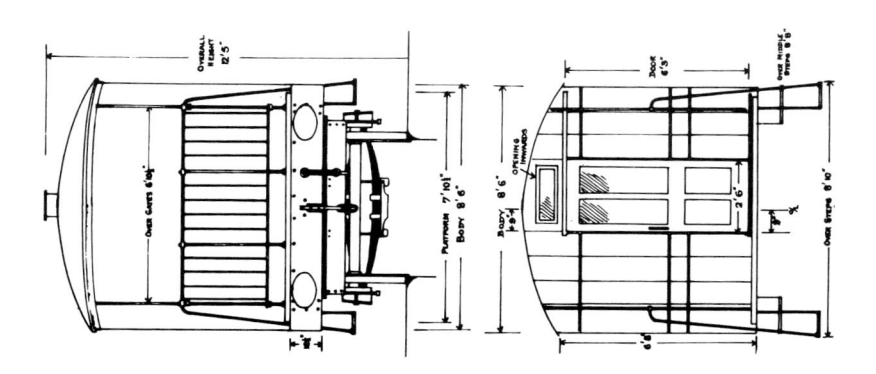

seated 50. The entrance doors from the platforms being off centre, the seat against the shorter side of the bulkead was for one only, that on the other side being for two. Externally the panelling was made up of vertical matchboarding.

Since no guard's compartment was provided in the bogie coaches, the trains ran for a time with a goods brake van attached, the three vehicles of this type being fitted specially with vacuum brake gear for this purpose. In 1909 two four-wheeled passenger brake vans were obtained from the same builders. The usual make-up of trains was then one third, one composite, and one brake. These brake vans were entirely different in construction, being built with horizontal boarding on wood framing 3" square, the framing being placed outside. Double doors were provided in the centre for the loading of parcels, and a separate door at one end for the guard. All doors had drop lights and louvre ventilators over. Both ends of the van were alike, having a lookout window at each side. Two gas lamps were provided, and vacuum brakes fitted, with guard's control cocks. There was also a hand screw brake.

Details of the numbering of this passenger stock have not survived, but it is believed that in the Knott End list the thirds were numbered 1–4, and the composites 5–8, while the brake vans were 9 and 10. One composite survived the massacre of Knott End stock after the passenger services were withdrawn in 1930, as did one brake van. This pair was drafted to the Wanlockhead branch of the former Caledonian Railway, and were there until the branch was closed in January 1939, when they were broken up. This particular composite was numbered 7899 in the second L.M.S. list (1934); the original 1923 renumbering is not known. On the Wanlockhead branch the coach acted as spare, a Sentinel railcar working most of the time.

10. GOODS ROLLING STOCK

By the time the L.M.S.R. took over, most of the Knott End goods stock consisted of comparatively modern wagons of various standard Railway Clearing House types, but one or two distinctive wagons still remained. In particular the three goods brake vans and some covered vans with peaked roofs, which had been altered from old 8-plank open wagons about 1912, specially for the salt traffic. An old employee of the railway averred that these wagons were very old, dating from the late seventies or early eighties, and that originally they had dumb

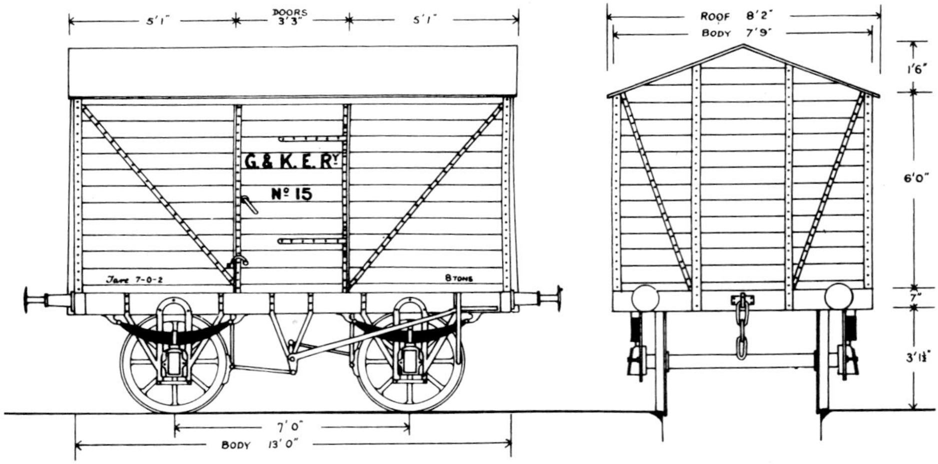
DOORS 3'3"
5'1"
5'1"
G. & K. E. R^Y
Nº 15
Tare 7-0-2
8 TONS
7'0"
BODY 13'0"
ROOF 8'2"
BODY 7'9"
1'6"
6'0"
7"
3'1½"

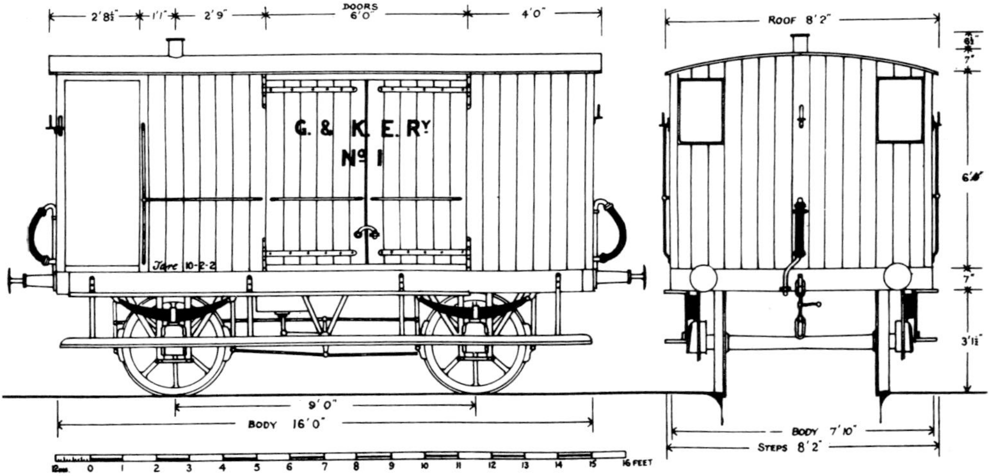
2'8½"
1'1"
2'9"
DOORS 6'0"
4'0"
G. & K. E. R^Y
Nº 1
Tare 10-2-2
9'0"
BODY 16'0"
ROOF 8'2"
6½"
7"
7"
3'1½"
BODY 7'10"
STEPS 8'2"
0 1 2 3 4 5 6 7 8 9 10 11 12 13 14 15 16 FEET

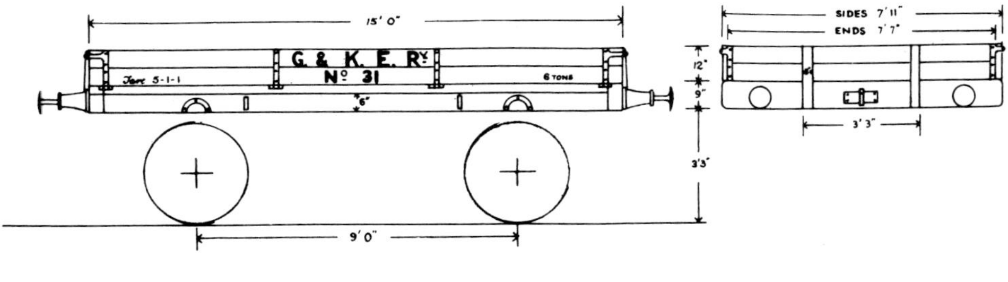
15'0"
G. & K. E. R^Y
Nº 31
Tare 5-1-1
6 TONS
6"
9'0"
SIDES 7'11"
ENDS 7'7"
12"
9"
3'3"
3'3"

The Garstang & Knott End Railway

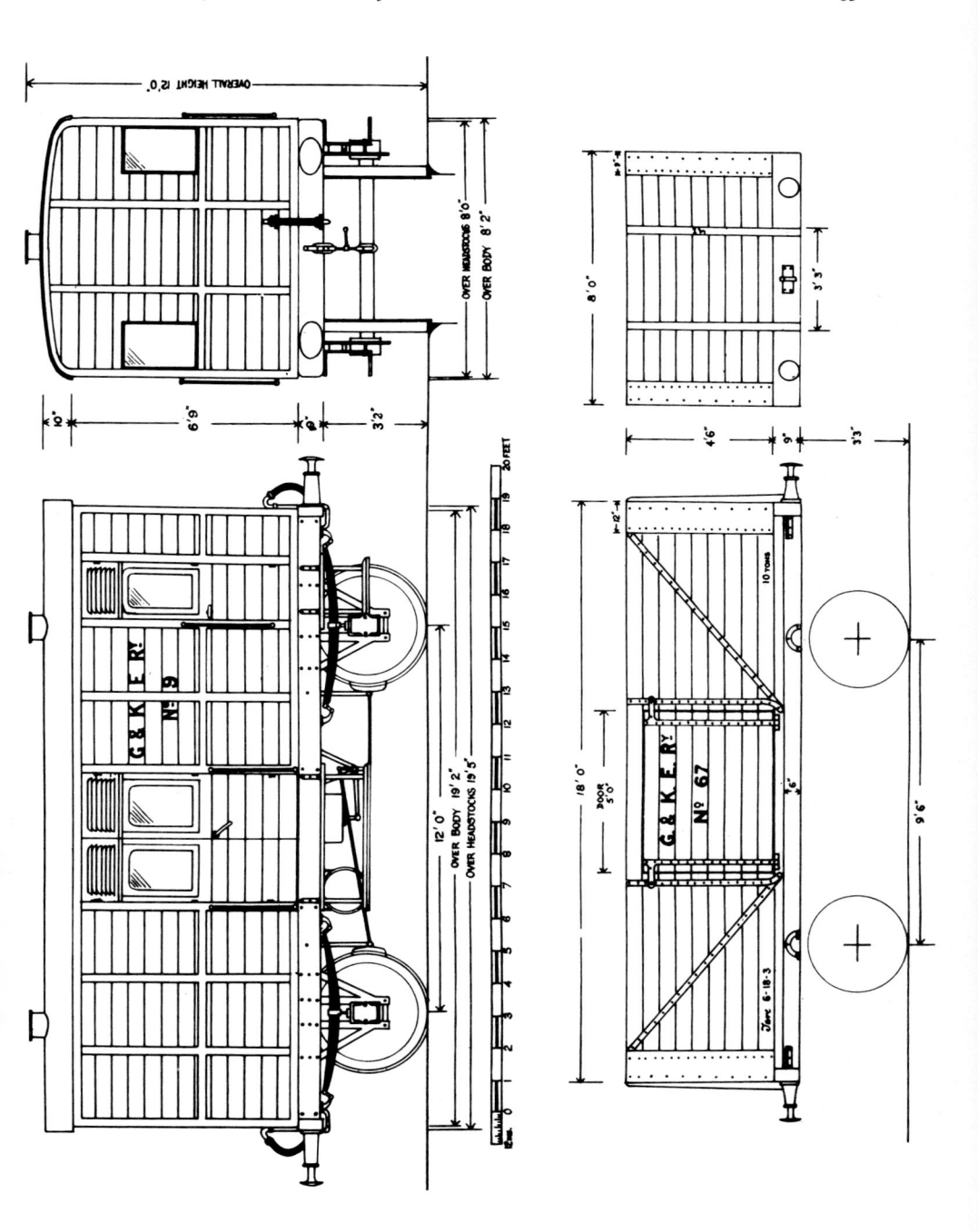

83

buffers. They were unusually short vehicles, of flush-sided construction with horizontal boarding and single centre doors. The end stanchions were faced with iron strapping, and were probably fitted as a strengthening measure when the wagons were rebuilt. The roof was felt covered. How many of these wagons there were is not now known, but only one or two survived until 1923, and they were broken up almost at once.

The three goods brake vans were 10-tonners, and were all of the same design. They had central double doors and a verandah at one end only, flush sided with vertical boarding and framing inside. Both ends were identical, except that the side lamp irons were fitted at the verandah end only. An unusual feature was that they were vacuum fitted, though no other goods stock had continuous brakes. This they acquired in 1908, for working with the passenger stock, as has been mentioned earlier. However, though brake van No. 1 retained its vacuum brake gear until after the grouping, that on the other two seems to have been removed sometime during the first World War.

Two other types of wagon in common use on the line are illustrated ; one a drop-side wagon of two planks, and six tons capacity and a ten-ton open wagon with side doors, both comparatively modern vehicles. Unfortunately no further information as to numbers and types of wagons is available, owing to the loss of records at Derby which was mentioned in the Preface to this book.

In the early days, the wagon stock, which consisted mainly of open wagons with a few covered vans for vegetable traffic, was fitted with smaller wheels than normal and had a buffer height of only three feet ; such as still remained in service in the period 1900–1909 were brought up to the modern standards by having larger wheels fitted and the buffer beams altered to bring the buffer height to 3′ 5″, so that they could be run through if necessary to places beyond Garstang on the L.N.W.R. system, as well as being standard with the new stock.

The G. & K.E.R. wagons did not last long under L.M.S. ownership, and were soon replaced by wagons from other sources, mainly L.N.W.R. and L. & Y.

11. LIVERY, AND SUNDRY NOTES

Of the livery of the four earlier locomotives, unfortunately nothing can be traced. One source suggests that " Union " was probably painted green, though there is no confirmation of this. From 1897,

Engine No. 44764 on a Pilling freight just on a curve north of Garstang Town. *M.R. Price*

Class 5 No. 44764 on a goods train at Cogie Hill Crossing in 1963. *M.R. Price*

however, we are on firmer ground, though again there are discrepancies in the various sources. The main colour is described as dark red, though this could mean anything from a brick red to a Midland lake, and nearer to that we cannot get. All four locomotives were in the same shade, though there were some variations in applying the lining and other embellishments. Smokeboxes, chimneys and underframes were black ; buffer beams were bright red. Wheels were black on the two Hudswell engines, and red on the Manning Wardle side tanks.

JUBILEE QUEEN, NEW CENTURY

Lining consisted of a fine yellow line with squared corners outside, and inside this a broad black line with rounded corners, edged on either side by a fine white line. This was on tanks, lower side panels of the cab and bunker. On the upper part of the cab sides and on the sandboxes, there was a fine yellow line only. The engine name was painted on the tank sides in 6" yellow letters, shaded blue. There was no indication of the owners' name on either of these engines.

KNOTT END

The lining here was slightly different, the outermost fine yellow line being omitted, and the broad black line edged with white had reversed rounded corners. On the tanks, the lining was carried round the front ends in one continuous panel. Though the owners were, strictly speaking, the Knott End Railway Co., the initials of the original company, G. & K.E.R., were painted on in yellow, with blue shading, low down on the tank sides at the front end. The name of the engine was on a brass plate, with raised letters and border, the background of the plate being painted red.

BLACKPOOL

Lining details were as for " Knott End," except for two minor points—the tank ends were treated as separate panels, and the initials G. & K.E.R. were at the rear of the tanks instead of the front. The dome cover of " Knott End " was originally polished brass, later painted over, while that of " Blackpool " was always painted.

PASSENGER STOCK

As far as can be ascertained, the 1870 coaches were painted brown, but exactly what shade is not stated. There appeared to be no lining of any description, and whether the vehicles were numbered or not is open to doubt. The new stock of 1908 was painted in a similar shade of red to the locomotives, and such lining as was put on was of a very simple character, being merely one long square-ended panel in yellow on the body below the waist. The coach number was carried low down at the extreme ends of the body, and the letters G. & K.E.R. on the narrow waist panel in the centre. Class designation, first or third, was painted on the waist panel of the entrance doors only. All lettering was in yellow, unshaded. Roofs were grey, and bogies and underframes black, as also was the ironwork. The raised mouldings on the panelling were the same colour as the body, and not picked out in any special way. The L.M.S.R. merely altered the lettering and numbers, only the one coach which migrated to Scotland ever being repainted in full L.M.S. livery.

The two passenger brake vans of 1909 were similar, but had no lining at all, and no lettering beyond the G. & K.E.R. initials and number.

GOODS STOCK

The whole of the stock was painted dark grey, with white lettering. Solebars were grey, but all running gear and other ironwork was black. For a period, commencing in 1908, the three goods brake vans were painted lake, owing to their use on passenger trains, but later reverted to the dark grey colour, though one report has it that No. 1, which retained the vacuum brake gear, was still in the red livery until 1921 at least.

BUILDINGS

There was no definite colour scheme for station buildings and other lineside structures. Wooden station buildings seem to have been painted a nondescript brown, or given a liberal coating of tar. In one or two cases, notably Garstang Town, the decor seems to have been mainly whitewash, this even extending to some brick buildings, including the goods shed. Corrugated iron was usually tarred, though in later years, it was generally in various shades of natural rust. Preesall station exhibited traces of green paint in its declining years. At Knott End, the woodwork appears to have been painted in some light colour, probably cream or stone, while the goods shed was whitewashed. Signal boxes, where they existed, were usually white in the upper parts, and brown below.

SIGNALLING

The early signalling installation—such as it was—was supplied by the long-defunct firm of Dutton & Co. As the line was built under Act of Parliament for passenger carrying, and not designated as a light railway (the Light Railways Act did not come into force until 1896) the Board of Trade insisted on full signalling. However, the company argued that as the line would be worked on the one-engine-in-steam principle, full signalling was not required under the regulations then in force. After some argument, the Board of Trade acquiesced, and as originally laid out, the line was signalled fully only until it had left the L.N.W.R. precincts at Garstang & Catterall, whence until Garstang Town was reached, no further signals were used. The signalling at Garstang Town consisted only of a starting signal for each direction, and Pilling had a starter only for the up line. These early signals were of the slotted-post variety. T. R. Perkins recorded in 1906 that the only signals remaining were a distant at Nateby and a small starter at Garstang Town.

Apart from Garstang & Catterall, where the eagle eye of the L.N.W.R. kept things up to scratch, the signalling gradually fell into disuse, and the electric telegraph was the sole means of control. Thus things remained, in spite of two engines being in use, until the opening of the extension to Knott End in 1908. As there were now at least three engines in regular daily use, the Board of Trade required full signalling and interlocking. There is some evidence that this was carried out between Pilling and Knott End, and partially only over the section between Garstang Town and Pilling, but by the end of 1919, it had degenerated. There were then starting signals only at Pilling and Knott End, though Garstang Town was fully signalled. At Knott End, in particular, only one signal was doing duty as starter for both platforms and the goods yard as well, and the interlocking had been taken out. How the company got away with this flagrant breach of regulations, is anybody's guess, but the fact remains that in spite of it all, there was never a fatal accident, after the "wagon jumping" episodes of 1870-1, and indeed nothing more serious than the occasional derailment throughout the railway's history.

When the L.M.S.R. took over, nothing was done (rather surprisingly) to alter the position, though the section from Garstang and Catterall to Garstang Town was brought up to main line standards, and so remains to this day. Beyond the Town station, things remained much as they were. After the withdrawal of passenger services in 1930, only the starting signals at Pilling and Knott End remained, and even these fell into disuse after a time. The signal boxes were dismantled and replaced by small ground frames, and the signalling instruments removed to the station buildings. Preesall and Nateby ceased to be block posts, and the passing loops at these places were disused. With the dismantling of the line beyond Pilling in 1950, there were two sections only—the junction to Garstang Town, and Garstang Town to

Pilling. Finally, with the reduction of the goods traffic to one train daily, there were no block posts, and the line was worked on the one-engine-in-steam principle again.

The Axe having now fallen on all sections of the line beyond Garstang Town, the pleasant countryside will no more hear the passing of the " Pilling Pig " as it approaches the level crossings, and the fields of Amounderness will revert to the unbroken solitudes of a century ago.

0-6-0 saddle tank *Jubilee Queen* seen here on the 29th September, 1939. *F. Moore Postcard*

The end of the line in 1963 is seen here at Pilling showing the old signal box and station house. *M.R.C. Price*

New Century photographed on 28th August 1923. *R. Kidner*

LOCOMOTIVES — DIMENSIONAL DETAILS

	Hebe	Union	Farmers' Friend	Hope	Jubilee Queen and New Century	Knott End	Blackpool
Cylinders … … …	13″ × 18″	9½″ × 14″	11″ × 17″	13″ × 20″	15″ × 20″	14″ × 20″	16″ × 22″
Wheels, Coupled … …	3′ 6″	2′ 9″	3′ 0″	3′ 6″	3′ 6″	4′ 0″	4′ 0″
„ Others … …	2′ 6″	—	—	—	—	—	2′ 9½″
Wheelbase … … …	5′ 6″ + 5′ 0″	5′ 0″	5′ 3″ + 5′ 3″	6′ 0″ + 6′ 0″	6′ 0″ + 6′ 0″	5′ 3″ + 5′ 3″	8′ 3″ + 6′ 0″ + 6′ 6″
„ Total …	10′ 6″	5′ 0″	10′ 6″	12′ 0″	12′ 0″	10′ 6″	20′ 9″
Boiler, Diameter … …	3′ 0″	2′ 11″	3′ 0″	3′ 0″	3′ 5″	3′ 11″	4′ 5″
„ Length … …	8′ 5½″	7′ 0″	8′ 4″	9′ 6″	9′ 3″	8′ 0″	10′ 0″
„ Centre Line …	5′ 0″	4′ 7″	4′ 11½″	5′ 6½″	5′ 8½″	6′ 6½″	8′ 0″
„ Pressure … …	140	120	120	120	140	150	150
„ Tubes … …	67 × 1⅞″	78 × 2″	—	81 × 2″	119 × 1½″	157 × 1¾″	180 × 1¾″
Heating Surface, Tubes …	289	286	—	403	593·45	556·4	832·4
„ „ Firebox…	32	33	—	61	67·04	52·6	69·6
„ „ Total …	321	319	—	464	660·49	610·0	902·0
Grate Area … …	6·5	9·5	—	10	10·62	10	14·5
Bunker Capacity (tons) …	¾	¾	—	1½	1½	1½	2
Tank Capacity (gallons) …	400	350	500	500	750	700	1000
Frame Length … …	17′ 8″	14′ 5½″	18′ 3″	20′ 7″	21′ 0″	23′ 0½″	29′ 11″
Overhang, Front (over buffer beams)	4′ 11″	4′ 10″	5′ 0″	5′ 10½″	6′ 0⅝″	6′ 6″	2′ 4″
„ Rear (over buffer beams)	3′ 0″	5′ 6″	3′ 8″	3′ 8½″	4′ 0⅝″	6′ 3″	7′ 0″
Length over Buffers …	21′ 2″	17′ 10″	22′ 8″	24′ 2″	24′ 4″	26′ 3″	33′ 0¼″
Chimney Height … …	10′ 0″	9′ 6″	10′ 0″	11′ 3″	10′ 8½″ *	11′ 6¾″	12′ 10″
Width, Cab Sides …	5′ 10″	5′ 6″	6′ 8″	7′ 0″	7′ 2″	8′ 0″	8′ 2″
„ Tanks … …	4′ 9″	4′ 6″	5′ 0″	5′ 0″	5′ 5″	8′ 0″	8′ 2″
„ Footplate … …	7′ 0″	6′ 0″	7′ 1½″	7′ 7¼″	7′ 10½″	8′ 6″	8′ 9″
„ Buffer Beams …	7′ 2½″	6′ 6″	7′ 5½″	7′ 7¼″	7′ 10½″	8′ 6″	8′ 9″
Tractive Effort (85%) …	7388	3905	5826	8208	12950	10413	14960
Builders … … …	B.H.	M.W.	H.C.	H.C.	H.C.	M.W.	M.W.
Works Number … …	118	226	173	263	484. 559	1732	1747
Date Built … … …	1870	1868	1875	1883	1897. 1900	1908	1909

*New Century—12′ 6″. B.H.—Black, Hawthorn & Co., Gateshead. H.C.—Hudswell, Clarke & Co., Leeds. M.W.—Manning, Wardle & Co., Leeds.

BIBLIOGRAPHY

" The Garstang & Knott End Railway "—Articles under this title in the *Railway Magazine*, as follows :

    By T. R. Perkins   January 1908
    By G. A. Sekon   December 1924
    By J. E. N. Ashworth   June 1930
    By F. S. Walmsley   December 1959

" The Garstang & Knott End Railway "—Article under this title by J. I. C. Boyd, in *Railway World*, July 1958.

" Windmill Land ", by Allen Clarke. (Foulsham & Co., 1933).

" The Making of the English Landscape—Lancashire ", by Roy Millward. (Hodder & Stoughton, 1955).

Ghosts of the Garstang & Knott End Railway (carriages especially). *Model Railway News*, October 1959.

Knott End and Garstang—1d. Guide published by the *Blackpool Times* in conjunction with the K.E. Railway, July 1908.